PERENNIALS

PERENNIALS

Oceana

AN OCEANA BOOK

This book is produced by
Quantum Publishing Ltd.
6 Blundell Street
London N7 9BH

ISBN 978-1-84573-348-3

QUMPGP2

Manufactured in Singapore by
Universal Graphics Pte. Ltd.
Printed in China by
L. Rex Printing Co. Ltd.

CONTENTS

INTRODUCTION

Billowing clouds of baby's breath, robust delphiniums reaching for the sky, translucent petals of poppies shimmering in the sun. These are a few of the images evoked by perennials in the garden. Perennials have provided generations of gardeners with a wealth of colours, shapes, textures and sizes of plants and flowers, with bloom spanning the seasons from hellebores pushing through snow in winter to the hardiest of the chrysanthemums persisting into the chilly days of autumn. With thousands of different perennial varieties available, the hardest part is narrowing the choices.

What exactly is a perennial? Basically, it is a plant that lives more than two years. As that description would also include trees and shrubs, the word is

further defined as being a plant that is herbaceous, or having soft, fleshy stems that die back in the autumn. There are a few exceptions to this, such as many of the ornamental grasses, semi-woody subshrubs and plants with evergreen foliage. While the foliage of most perennials dies each year, the roots are able to survive varying degrees of winter cold and send up new growth in the spring. A perennial may be able to do this for several years or for decades, depending on many factors.

Besides true perennials, certain biennial plants are included in this book. Biennials take two years to complete their life cycle: in the first year from seed they produce only leaves, and in the second they grow and bloom, set seed and die.

USING PERENNIALS IN THE GARDEN

The most traditional way to use perennials is in borders, with the plants placed either in ribbon-like bands or in natural clumps. Except in very formal, geometric gardens, the latter method is generally preferred. Often, two parallel borders are developed, separated by a lawn, a path or both. A fence, hedge or wall is often included as a backdrop. Free-standing beds, either in geometric shapes or in less formal undulating designs, are another way to use perennials in the landscape. Such beds are intended to be viewed from all sides.

The wealth of perennials available from around the world is also useful in many other ways in the landscape. A group of trees underplanted with a variety of ferns and other shade-loving perennials becomes a woodland garden. Perennials native to alpine areas or regions with dry, gravelly soil are the best ones to choose in softening the harsh lines of a stone wall or making a rocky outcropping into a rock garden. A wet, marshy area beside a stream or pool turns into a bog garden when planted with perennials that tolerate very moist conditions. An open expanse of lawn is transformed into a glorious meadow garden when filled with brightly-coloured flowers and ornamental grasses that thrive in these conditions.

Perennials can also provide an accent in the landscape, or, when planted in containers, turn a terrace or patio into a flower-filled retreat.

GROWING CONDITIONS

As you begin the process of deciding what perennials you want to grow, first consider your growing conditions. These factors include minimum winter temperatures, soil, light and water.

Hardiness is mainly determined by the ability of a plant to survive a minimum winter temperature. Water and soil conditions plus other factors also play a role. These work together so that even within a small garden there will be such microclimatic differences that a plant may survive in one corner but not in another. For example, temperatures will be lower at the bottom of a hill, on the north side of a house or in an area exposed to wind. Good drainage is a key element, for should water be allowed to collect around roots and then freeze, the results are usually fatal. With experience, you will learn which areas are best for certain plants. You may even be able to find that extra warm spot for growing a plant that is not normally hardy in your area.

Although some perennials must have full sun, there are a great number that tolerate either full sun or light shade, plus others that grow best in light or even full shade. In regions with hot, humid summers, light or partial shade is often necessary for plants to survive. This may be provided by planting on the east or west side of a building, hedge or fence so that sun is received for at least four to six hours each day. The lightly dappled shade beneath open trees is similar; this can be created by thinning out upper branches or trimming off lower

ABOVE: An area shaded in the afternoon provides the ideal growing conditions for plants intolerant of heat or those that need light shade, such as this planting of hostas, astilbes (*above*), Solomon's seal and ferns.

ones. When choosing a lightly shaded site, one that gets morning sun and afternoon shade is usually the best option.

Heavily dappled shade under trees, the dense shade on the north side of a building, hedge or fence, or any position with four hours or less of sun each day is considered full shade. Very few perennials bloom well in these conditions, but there are a number with beautiful foliage suitable for these areas.

ABOVE: A quick way of determining your soil type is to pick up a handful, squeeze, then poke the soft ball with your fingers. If it crumbles easily, then you probably have the best – a loam soil.

For most perennials, the ideal soil, called loam, has a balanced mixture of sand, silt and clay particles, drains well, and has a generous supply of organic matter, or humus. Fortunately, organic matter can make either sandy soil that drains too quickly or clay soil that drains slowly quite amenable, because it helps to retain water and nutrients while at the same time allowing air spaces around the plant roots. An additional benefit is that it enhances the growth of soil microorganisms that release plant nutrients. The most common sources of organic matter are peat moss, compost or leaf-mould.

To determine your soil type quickly, dig up a handful of soil three to five days after a rainfall and squeeze. If it forms a ball that does not readily break apart it is probably high in clay; a loose gritty soil is mainly sand, while a soil ball that crumbles loosely is a loam. To determine drainage, dig a hole 30 cm (12 in) deep and fill with water. If the water has not seeped away in an hour, the drainage is poor. If the poor drainage is due to a clay soil, adding organic matter is usually enough, but if it is due to other factors such as a hardpan, or impervious layer, beneath the top soil, then growing plants in raised beds or containers, or installing

drainage tiles should be considered.

Most plants grow best with an average of 2.5 cm (1 in) of rainfall or irrigation each week during the growing season. In choosing which plants to grow in your garden, consider either the natural rainfall or your willingness to supplement it. The use of a mulch helps to conserve soil moisture.

For a lot of people, choosing plants with low-maintenance qualities is of prime importance. Some plants must be staked, others need to be divided frequently, pinched back, have faded flowers removed, be sprayed for pests or other time-consuming chores.

ABOVE: For a garden with an abundance of shade there are perennial flowers and plants that will turn a dull area into one with a wealth of texture and form. Gardening in the shade is not as easy as gardening in the sun and hostas (*above*) are ideal as they favour a shady spot.

Developing a design

Once you have established your growing conditions and considered the possible perennials, you are ready to develop a design. Borders are usually best if at least 1.20 m (4 ft) wide and beds at least 1.80 m (6 ft) at their widest. If there is a hedge behind a border, provide 60 cm (2 ft) of space between. A border is intended to be viewed from one, two or three sides, so place taller plants at the back with progressively shorter ones towards the front. With free-standing beds, place the tallest plants in the middle with plants of gradually decreasing heights towards the outer edges. Breaking this guideline occasionally helps to prevent monotony, and a group of tall plants in the front of a bed or border has a bold, dynamic effect. Placing some of the low-growing, spring-blooming plants towards the centre of a bed or border makes it more interesting too.

The season of bloom and growth habit of the plants are also to be considered. Some people may be satisfied with a perennial garden that is in bloom for a specific time of the year, while others want one border to be flowering for as much of the growing season as possible. Generally, using smaller plants in a compact garden and larger plants in a bigger garden is recommended; this guideline is best broken when a large, strongly architectural plant is used in a small garden for a dramatic accent.

In developing flower beds and borders, do not limit yourself strictly to perennials. Combining bulbs, annuals, herbs and shrubs within a strong framework of perennials will provide greater possibilities for colour, form and texture, and a longer blooming season, plus more interest in the winter months.

Studying a colour wheel is helpful in combining colours. Basically, remember that reds, oranges and yellows are warm colours and greens, blues and violets are cool colours, with the former implying feelings of excitement and passion and the latter tranquillity and calm. Cool

ABOVE: Complementary colour schemes utilize colours opposite on the colour wheel, with the most popular combination being purple and yellow, such as yellow helianthus (*left*) and purple primula (*right*).

colours tend to appear farther away from the viewer, while warm colours appear closer. This effect can be used to create illusions. Cool colours planted at the back of the garden make it seem larger, while a border of warm-coloured flowers makes it seem smaller. Unfortunately, since cool colours recede, they tend to lose their impact far away and are best observed close-up. In combining warm and cool colours, warm colours are best used more sparingly as they can easily overwhelm the cooler-coloured flowers.

In developing colour schemes, it is helpful to understand that a pure colour is called a hue, a tint is lighter and a shade is darker. There are four basic colour schemes. Monochromatic schemes utilize flowers in various tints and shades of one colour. In a garden, green is always present, so a truly monochromatic garden is not possible. Analogous schemes usually utilize the tints and shades of three adjoining colours on the colour wheel, such as yellow, yellow-orange and orange. Complementary schemes combine colours that are opposite on the colour wheel, such as orange and blue, or yellow and violet. These are difficult to achieve successfully, but by using pure hues, including white flowers or foliage, and intermingling plants, they can be very powerful. Polychromatic schemes combine any and every colour; the result can be garish or pleasing.

Plant form is another important design consideration. The five basic forms of perennials are rounded, vertical, open, upright and spreading and prostrate. Beds and borders may be composed of only one form, the repetition of several forms, combinations of complementary forms or a mixture of all the forms.

Texture refers to the appearance of the plant, not to how it actually feels to the touch. The terms fine, medium and coarse are determined by the size and density of the foliage and flowers. As with colour, spatial illusions can be created with texture. Plants with coarse texture appear closer, and fine-textured ones seem further away. Coarse-textured plants at the back of the garden make the garden seem smaller, and fine-textured ones in a narrow border make it appear wider.

Once you have analysed your site, considered the design basics and made a list of plants you want to include, you are ready to draw a garden plan. Drawing a plan to scale on graph paper will help you to get a sense of the space and proportions as well as the number of plants needed. Determine the dimensions of the site and outline the shape of the bed or border on the graph paper. From your list of plants, begin drawing in the clumps of plants on a sheet of tracing paper laid over the graph paper; include as many of the plant characteristics, usually in code, as needed to help you to have an accurate picture of the garden. For example, you might want information about height, form, colour and season of bloom. Overlaying layers of tracing paper can help in experimenting with different combinations or seeing how the garden will look at different seasons. Use coloured pencils or markers to indicate colours, if desired. Unless the garden is very small, placing at least three of the same plants together gives the greatest impact.

PREPARING THE SOIL

Since the perennial garden is intended to bring lasting pleasure, adequate preparation of the soil before planting is worth every bit of effort. If the area is large or you are unfamiliar with the pH and nutrient levels in your garden, have the soil tested at a laboratory or use one of the simple soil test kits that are available from garden centres.

Soil can be damaged by digging when it is too wet, so wait until it is partially dry. Remove any large stones and compost the sod. For best results, use a spade or fork to turn the soil over to a depth of 30–45 cm (12–18 in); alternatively, rototill the soil as deeply as possible. Spread a 5–7.5 cm (2–3 in) layer of organic matter evenly on top. Sprinkle on lime to adjust pH, according to soil test recommendations, and granular or timed-release fertilizer, again according to test recommendations or directions on the package label. An average recommendation is 2.5–2.25 kg (3–5 lb) of a phosphorus-rich fertilizer or 4.5 kg (10 lb) of commercially dried cow or sheep manure per 9 sq m (100 square ft). Using a spade or rototiller, work these ingredients into the soil. Rake the surface smooth.

MULCHING

The idea of a mulch is to add a layer of insulation on top of the soil, preventing sudden changes in soil temperature, changes that can wreak havoc to the root systems of tender plants. Regions with reliable snow cover already enjoy the advantages of a natural snow mulch – nature's insulation. However, where snow is unreliable, a late autumn mulch can help in certain cases.

Mulching materials should be organic matter that remains loose and won't pack down to suffocate your plants. Good choices might be dried leaves, clean straw, chopped dead tops from other perennials or evergreen boughs from pruning. Mulch can be simply piled high on top of your plants, but a depth of 15–20 cm (6–8 in) or more is ideal.

BUYING AND PLANTING PERENNIALS

Perennial plants may be purchased locally at garden centres and nurseries, usually in 10 cm (4 in) or 3.75 litre (1 gallon) pots. Most of these plants will be old enough to bloom the first year. Select plants that are busy and compact, with healthy green foliage and no sign of insects or diseases.

There are a great number of mail-order companies offering seed, while others ship young seedling plants, dormant bare-root plants or older, larger plants in pots. Some companies are specialists in rare and unusual varieties. Many have colourful catalogues filled with detailed facts about the different plants, providing a valuable source of information. Most companies are reliable, but if you have never ordered by mail before, talk with other gardeners to learn about their experiences. Spring catalogues are mailed in the middle of winter. Plants ordered then will be shipped in early spring as dormant bare-root plants, or later in containers.

If possible, plant on a day that is cool and cloudy, with rain predicted in a day or so. Planting in late afternoon is better than in the morning. Avoid hot or windy weather.

When planting dormant bare-root perennials, the roots should not dry out, so place small stakes at the proper spacings in the prepared soil, and unwrap and plant each one individually. With a trowel dig a hole large enough so the roots spread out. Except as noted in the Encyclopedia Section, set the point where the roots meet the stem or crown at ground level. Fill in with soil around the roots and tamp gently. Then water thoroughly.

Although container-grown plants can be planted at any time they are purchased during the growing season, planting in spring after the last frost is preferred. Rather than using stakes to mark planting spots, you can set the pots out and move them around until satisfied. When ready to plant, dig a hole, gently remove the plant from the pot, loosen the roots slightly with your fingers or cut them with a knife if they are very thick, and set into the hole. The soil level should be just slightly higher than in the pot, as the plant will settle. Then water thoroughly.

ABOVE: Ramonda mayconi

Taking care of your perennials

Fertilizing

In nature, plants rely on sunlight, rain and the nutrients in the soil. Nature limits the types and numbers of plants by the relative amounts of these basics available. In our landscapes, we grow many plants together with differing requirements, often in a variety of types of soil, surrounded with competing grass. If they are to thrive, we have to supplement what Nature can provide.

A complete fertilizer contains nitrogen, phosphorus and potassium. The percentage of these elements, always in the order above, is described by the three numbers on the package, such as 5–10–10. Most perennials grown for their blooms do best with a fertilizer lower in nitrogen than the other two elements, as nitrogen benefits foliage growth at the expense of flowers. Fertilizer may be applied in granular form, timed-release pellets or as a liquid.

Additional fertilizer is not necessary in the first year of planting if the area is well-prepared, although a light feeding in midsummer would be all right. In subsequent years, feed once in the spring with about 1 kg (2 lb) of a phosphorus-rich fertilizer per 9 sq m (100 square ft) and again in midsummer. Liquid fertilizers are especially good for spot feeding those plants that are heavy feeders or those that seem to need an extra boost.

Watering

Perennials need summer watering, preferably infrequent deep waterings. Apply an inch of water each week, or as needed, depending on soil type. Although most perennials tolerate average soil, or one that briefly dries out, a great many perennials thrive in a soil that remains evenly moist but is never soggy. If natural rainfall does not provide this, supplemental watering is necessary.

The best method is to use a rubber, plastic or canvas soaker hose laid among the plants. Water in the morning so the foliage has a chance to dry off before nightfall, as dampness encourages the spread of disease organisms. Soak the soil thoroughly; it should be moist 7.5–10 cm (3–4 in) deep.

WEEDING AND MULCHING

Weeds are inevitable in any garden. Try to pull them while they are still young before they get deep roots or flower and set seed. Try not to disturb the roots of the perennials. If a large clump of soil is removed when weeding, bring in additional topsoil from another part of the garden.

Adding a layer of organic mulch helps to keep weeds in check. It also slows down the evaporation of moisture from the soil, keeps the soil cool, that encourages root growth and adds humus to the soil as it decomposes. In spring after removing any weeds, apply a layer of mulch several centimetres (inches) thick over the surface of beds and borders, tapering it thinly near the perennials. Some of the possible organic mulches include partly decayed leaves, rotted compost, chopped bracken, bark chippings, straw, spent hops, moistened peat, lawn mowings and well-decayed manure.

ABOVE: Mulching with a several-centimetre (inch) layer of organic material, such as this partially composted ground bark and tree limbs, is beneficial in several ways. It helps the soil to retain moisture for longer, reduces the need for watering, deters weeds, keeps the soil cool and adds vital organic material to the soil.

STAKING

There are two types of staking needs: for the tall, single-stalked plants, such as delphinium, foxglove and monkshood, and for plants with thin, floppy stems, such as yarrow, aster, chrysanthemum and coreopsis.

Use bamboo stakes or wooden poles for the tall plants, inserting each one 30 cm (12 in) into the ground and 2.5 cm (1 in) from the stalk. Use a plant tie or twine to attach the stalk to the stake

ABOVE: Stake single-stemmed tall plants, such as delphinium, with bamboo, wood or metal stalks set 30 cm (1 ft) deep and tied loosely to the plant at several points along the stem.

loosely. If the tie is too tight, the plant will be injured.

Bushy, thin-stemmed plants can be staked with any of several types of purchased supports or by encircling the plant with twiggy tree branches 45–60 cm (18–24 in) long. When the plant is half that height, insert several branches into the soil around the plant. As the season progresses, the foliage will hide the twigs.

PINCHING, THINNING AND DISBUDDING

Pinching out the growing tip from a plant forces side branches to grow more readily, making plants shorter, sturdier, bushier and grow more flowers. Use your fingers to remove a small amount of the growth. This is usually done several times before the beginning of July. Chrysanthemums need this treatment but other perennials such as phlox and asters benefit as well.

Some perennials including phlox, delphiniums, sneezewort, Shasta daisies and asters, produce so many shoots that growth is spindly and air circulation is poor, which promotes fungus diseases. Thinning out some of the stalks when growth is 10–15 cm (4–6 in) tall will reduce this problem.

Disbudding, or removing some of the flower buds, allows the remaining bud to produce an extra large flower. Remove the small side buds early in development, if desired, on such plants as peonies, hibiscus and large-flowered chrysanthemums.

DEADHEADING

A relatively self-explanatory term, deadheading refers to cutting off the dead, or faded, flowers. This not only makes the garden neater and cleaner, but also prevents seed development. This is often desirable because seed development can weaken the plant, cause it to stop blooming, or allow it to re-seed and become a nuisance. Often, the seedlings are of inferior quality to the parent, especially if the latter is a hybrid or other cultivar. With some early-blooming plants, such as lupin, phlox, camomile and delphinium, removing the faded flowers makes the plants bloom again in late summer or autumn.

WINTER PROTECTION

After several frosts have killed back plants, cut off the dead stems to 5–10 cm (2–4 in). Removing this debris from the garden not only makes it look more attractive during the winter, but it also reduces the places where pests can overwinter.

A winter mulch protects tender plants and prevents shallow-rooted perennials from being heaved out of the ground through alternate freezing and thawing of the soil. To apply, wait until the ground has frozen to a depth of 5 cm (2 in) and plants are completely dormant. Then, spread a 7.5–15 cm (3–6 in) layer of loose, open mulch, such as oak leaves, light pine branches or straw around the plants. This layer can be thicker for extra-tender perennials.

ABOVE: Lupinus 'Queen of Hearts'

STARTING PERENNIALS FROM SEED

ABOVE: Hibiscus trionum

Most gardeners either buy their perennials from local or mail-order nurseries, or get plants from other gardeners. Starting perennials from seed is much less usual, except for certain plants that readily grow this way. These include English daisy, delphiniums, pinks, hibiscus, foxgloves, gloriosa daisies, lupins, Shasta daisy and painted daisy.

The procedure is much the same as starting annual seeds indoors or in a greenhouse, except that there is often a two-year wait before the plants bloom. This long lag time necessitates developing a nursery area for growing the plants until they can be in the garden as well as protecting them during the winter.

Perennials have differing germination requirements, so follow the instructions on the seed packet. Use any of the specialized equipment for starting seeds, such as peat moss cubes or pellets, or peat pots, plastic pots, trays or cell-packs filled with moistened seed compost. Sow the seeds, then handle according to the specific requirements on the packet. Some perennial seeds must have heat or light to germinate, while others need cool temperatures or darkness. Sometimes the seed coats must have special treatment, such as being nicked with a file or having boiling water poured over them. The germination time varies greatly as well. Whatever the procedure, be sure to keep the growing medium moist. Once the seeds germinate, provide bright, indirect light, either by growing under fluorescent lights, or placing in a greenhouse.

After several sets of leaves have developed, transplant the seedlings to larger pots or into a nursery bed. Shelter them with cloches or continue growing in a cool greenhouse or indoors under lights for several weeks until they are actively growing again. At this time, transplant to a nursery area outdoors. Water and feed regularly during the summer. Mulch the nursery bed in late autumn after the ground has frozen or cover with a cold frame.

LEFT: Delphinium grandiflorum

DIVIDING PERENNIALS

As perennials spread and grow, each plant competes with itself and other plants for water, nutrients and space. Dividing perennials, then, is a significant part of their upkeep. Division is needed either to rejuvenate an ageing plant, to control the size of a plant or to have additional plants.

Spring- and summer-blooming plants are generally divided in late summer or autumn and autumn-blooming plants in early spring. In areas with winters of –28°C (–20°F) or colder, division is often best accomplished in the spring, so plants have a full growing season to become established before facing the rigours of winter; the exception are the plants blooming in early spring, such as primroses, leopard's bane and lungwort.

Several days previously, water the bed well. For spring division, plan on keeping two to four beds or sprouts with each section; when dividing in autumn or whenever in active growth, cut the plants back by half and keep at least two to four stems with each portion.

With a large fork or spade, dig up the entire clump. If possible, use your hands to divide the clump into smaller sections. When roots are tightly ensnarled, insert two large forks back to back in the centre and press the handles towards each other, prising the clump apart. For plants with thick, carrot-like roots, use a knife to cut apart each section. If the centre of the clump has not died, it is sometimes possible to use a spade to cut away portions at the outer edges of the plant.

Replenish the soil in the hole from which the clump was removed with top soil, organic matter and a handful of nitrogen-free fertilizer. Replant one or more of the divisions in the hole, if desired, and replant the others in another part of the garden. Keep the plants well watered until established again.

PROPAGATING FROM STEM AND ROOT CUTTINGS

Using stem cuttings for propagation is an efficient way to get additional plants without digging up the parent plant. Generally, spring is the best time to take stem cuttings of summer-blooming plants, and early summer is best for plants blooming in spring and autumn.

To take a cutting, cut a piece 10–20 cm (4–8 in) long from the top of a stalk. It is best to cut slightly below the point where leaves join the stem. Remove the lower leaves, moisten the stem end, dip in rooting hormone and put in a pot of moistened seed compost. Insert a label showing the date and the name of the plant, and cover the pot with a plastic bag. Place in a warm spot with bright, indirect light. Do not let the seed compost dry out; mist the cuttings several times a day. When cuttings have rooted and new growth starts, transplant to bigger pots or to a nursery bed. When plants are large enough, transfer to the garden.

Root cuttings are mainly useful when a large number of plants are wanted. It works best with just a few perennials. In early spring, either cut off some of the outer roots without disturbing the plant or dig up the entire plant and cut up all or part of the roots.

For plants with fine roots, such as phlox, yarrow, sea holly, spurge, blanket flower, salvia and Stokes' aster, cut the roots into pieces 5 cm (2 in) long and spread them horizontally over the surface of a tray of moistened potting compost. Cover them with 1.27 cm (½ in) more of moist compost. Keep moist until the sprouts develop, then treat the plants as seedlings.

For plants with fleshy roots, such as bee balm, bleeding heart, baby's breath, poppies and peonies, cut the roots into pieces 5–7.5 cm (2–3 in) long, keeping the top ends facing the same direction. Plant them vertically, top ends up, in moistened potting compost with 0.6 cm (¼ in) sticking above the soil. Keep moist until sprouts develop, then treat as seedlings.

HOW TO USE THIS BOOK

The perennials chosen for this include ones that have been favourites for generations as well as those that have only recently come into garden use. Besides popularity, the length of time each year the plant makes an aesthetic contribution to the garden was also considered. A plant should either bloom for a long period or be attractive for most of the growing season. Conversely, if the foliage does become unattractive, then it should die down quickly so other plants fill in.

- Perennials are arranged alphabetically by their botanical, or Latin binomial name.

- Accompanying each entry is a key reference panel providing vital information.

Species, variety or cultivar:
   hybrid cultivar
Other common names:
   Bear's Breeches
Height and spread:
   90 x 150 m (3 x 5ft)
Blooming period:
   Summer
Soil type:
   Moist, well-drained, humus-rich soil
Sun or Shade:
   Likes a sunny spot but does well in partial shade
Hardiness:
   Minimum temp −23°C (−10°F)

DEFINING BOTANICAL TERMS

Both the common and the botanical, or Latin binomial, names have been used in the plant descriptions. Just as a person's full name is necessary for proper identification, the same applies to plants. A common name for a plant in one region may be used for an entirely different plant somewhere else while Latin names are the same throughout the world.

A binomial includes the generic name, which is followed by the species name. Sometimes there is a third word, which is a subspecies or variety (var.) name. Taxonomists sometimes change botanical names, and the older forms have been included for clarification. A garden form, sport, clone or result of a hybrid cross is called a cultivar; the cultivar name is enclosed in single quotation marks. Cultivars are usually propagated vegetatively, from divisions or cuttings, as they may or may not reproduce true from seed.

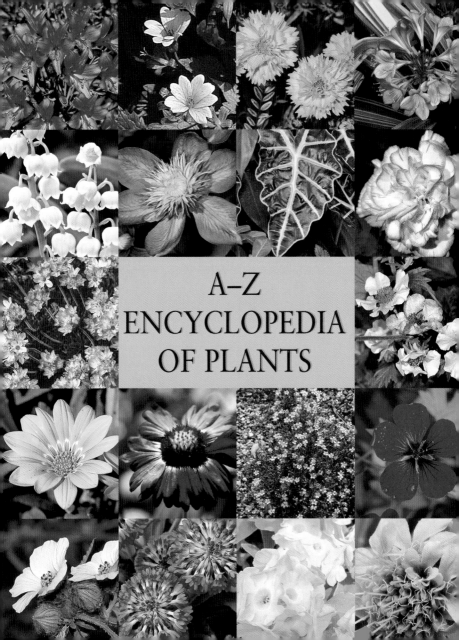

A–Z
ENCYCLOPEDIA
OF PLANTS

Acanthus spinosus • *Bear's Breeches*

DESCRIPTION

Classified within the Acanthaceae family, this genus includes 30 species of perennials and subshrubs from the temperate and tropical Old World regions. The acanthus leaf was the basis for many classical Greek and Roman designs, and was often featured atop columns and along friezes. Early Christians adopted the leaf as a symbol of heaven.

A. *spinosus* is found in regions around the Mediterranean and has deeply divided, broad, spiny leaves that form a basal clump, and white, sometimes mauve-tinted tubular flowers in shiny bracts. 'Lady Moore' has purple and white flowers and variegated leaves. They self-sow freely and can sucker, with large seed pods following, and although cold tolerant, they prefer mild winters.

Species, variety or cultivar:
 'Lady Moore'
Other common names:
 Bear's Breeches
Height and spread:
 90 x 150 cm (3 x 5 ft)
Blooming period:
 Summer
Soil type:
 Moist, well-drained, humus-rich soil
Sun or Shade:
 Likes a sunny spot but does well in partial shade
Hardiness:
 Minimum temp –23°C (–10°F)

Achillea x kellereris • *Yarrow*

DESCRIPTION

This genus of about 100 species of clumping or mat-forming perennial plants is a member of the large daisy (Asteraceae) family, and grows throughout Europe and northern and western Asia in a range of habitats including alpine. The foliage is usually finely divided with a fern-like appearance and is often aromatic. The flowerheads are flattened or umbel-like, comprising numerous small flowers in white and pale cream, lemon and pink. Numerous cultivars are available in brighter shades and these make excellent border plants. Most species are easily grown in well-drained soil in full sun. They can tolerate quite poor conditions but alpine species require perfect drainage and protection from winter rain if downy-leafed. Propagation is by division or from seed.

A. x kellereri is a garden hybrid of *A. clypeolata* and *A. ageratifolia*, and forms mats of ferny grey foliage. Small heads of creamy white daisy-like flowers with pale yellow centres are borne in summer. Suitable for rock gardens.

ABOVE: *Achillea ageratifolia* (common name Greek yarrow). A low-growing, mat-forming plant which features small, flattish, white flower clusters.

LEFT: *Achillea clypeolata* (common name Yarrow) originates from the Balkans and has golden-yellow flowers, but it is really the foliage that stands out.

Species, variety or cultivar:
    –
Other common names:
    Yarrow
Height and spread:
    15 x 25 cm (6 x 10 in)
Blooming period:
    Summer
Soil type:
    Well-drained soil
Sun or Shade:
    Sun or shade
Hardiness:
    Minimum temp –29°C (–20°F)

Achillea millefolium · *Yarrow*

DESCRIPTION

A. millefolium is a weedy species native to
Europe and western Asia and grows in a
range of habitats, including alpine. It can
tolerate quite poor conditions, and has
naturalized in numerous temperate regions.
The lush green foliage is finely divided with a
fern-like appearance, and is slightly aromatic.
Flattened flowerheads comprising numerous
small dull white flowers appear from summer
through to autumn. Propagation is by division
or from seed, but care should be taken as this
species is too invasive for most gardens. There
are many fine cultivars however, in a range of
attractive colours, and ideal for garden use,
such as 'Paprika'.

Species, variety or cultivar::
  'Paprika'
Other common names:
  Milfoil, Yarrow
Height and spread:
  75 x 75 cm (30 x 30 in)
Blooming period:
  Summer to autumn
Soil type:
  Well-drained soil
Sun or Shade:
  Prefers full sun
Hardiness:
  Minimum temp –40°C (–40°F)

Aconitum napellus • *Friar's Cup*

DESCRIPTION

This buttercup (Ranunculaceae) family genus of around 100 species of often tuberous biennials and perennials is found in northern temperate zones. Completely dormant over winter, they quickly develop a clump of deeply lobed fan-shaped leaves from which

emerge erect stems bearing clusters of pendulous, hooded or helmet-shaped flowers, usually white, creamy yellow or mauve-blue, to purple in colour.

A. napellus is found in Europe, Asia and North America, and is an upright perennial with dark green slightly hairy leaves and five to seven toothed lobes. Bright purple-blue helmet-shaped flowers in dense heads atop tall stems are borne from late summer–autumn.

Species, variety or cultivar:
–
Other common names:
Friar's Cap, Helmet Flower, Monkshood
Height and spread:
1.8 x 0.8 m (72 x 32 in)
Blooming period:
Summer to autumn
Soil type:
Moist, humus-rich, well-drained soil
Sun or Shade:
Likes both full sun and part-sun
Hardiness:
Minimum temp –29°C (–20°F)

Agapanthus praecox • *African Lily*

DESCRIPTION

This southern African genus consists of ten species of fleshy-rooted perennials of the onion (Alliaceae) family. Long, strappy, fleshy leaves form dense clumps of evergreen or deciduous foliage. *A. praecox* has fleshy bright green leaves to 70 cm (27 in) long, and wide-opening, pale to mid-blue flowers on stems to 90 cm (36 in) tall. It is the most widely cultivated species in warm-temperate gardens, and will withstand drought and poor soil, but has better flower production with good conditions. Slugs and snails often damage young foliage. Propagate by division in winter or raise from seed.

Species, variety or cultivar:
–
Other common names:
African Lily, Lily-of-the-Nile
Height and spread:
100 x 130 cm (40 x 50 in)
Blooming period:
Summer
Soil type:
Well-drained soil
Sun or Shade:
Enjoys full sun
Hardiness:
Minimum temp –7°C (20°F)

Agastache • *Giant Hyssop*

DESCRIPTION

There are 20 species of very aromatic perennials in this genus, which belongs to the mint (Lamiaceae) family. They are native to North America, China and Japan where they grow in dry scrub and fields. Flowers may be red, orange, rose, violet, blue or white and are typically tubular with two lips. They are borne in densely packed whorls on spikes or narrow panicles in summer and are very popular with bees. Some species are used in herbal medicines and teas.

The crossing of several species has resulted in a range of hybrid cultivars of varying heights and colours, including 'Blue Fortune,' which has bluish purple flowers.

Species, variety or cultivar:
  hybrid cultivar, 'Blue Fortune'
Other common names:
  Giant Hyssop, Mexican Hyssop
Height and spread:
  1.8 x 0.9 m (6 x 3 ft)
Blooming period:
  Summer
Soil type:
  Well-drained soil
Sun or Shade:
  Prefers full sun
Hardiness:
  Minimum temp −18°C (0°F)

Ajania pacifica • *Pacific Gold*

DESCRIPTION

A genus of 30 perennial herbs or shrubs from the daisy (Asteraceae) family, native to central and eastern Asia. Corymbs or racemes of daisy-like flowers, arranged in a radial pattern, appear in autumn. Spreading by underground fleshy stems, these hardy plants adapt to exposed positions or partial shade, and require a well-drained, moderately fertile soil, which should be kept moist. Propagate them from seed or by division.

A. *pacifica* is a drought-tolerant perennial from far-eastern Russia and northern Japan, which forms a spreading mound of dark green, scalloped, felt-like leaves, with white edges and silver undersides. It is covered in clusters of yellow daisy-like flowers in autumn.

Species, variety or cultivar:
–

Other common names:
Pacific Gold and Silver Chrysanthemum

Height and spread:
45 x 30 cm (18 x 12 in)

Blooming period:
Autumn

Soil type:
Well-drained, moderately fertile soil, kept moist

Sun or Shade:
Likes full sun to part-shade

Hardiness:
Minimum temp –29°C (–20°F)

Alchemilla speciosa • *Bear's Foot*

DESCRIPTION

A widespread Eurasian genus in the rose (Rosaceae) family of around 300 species of clump-forming soft-stemmed perennials. Alchemilla has featured in herbal medicine, mainly in poultices to stop bleeding and encourage healing, but also in elixirs of youth.

A. speciosa is from the Caucasus, and is a mounding spreading species with hairy flower stems and deeply-lobed toothed leaves, which are finely hairy above and very hairy below. Sprays of yellow-green flowers appear in summer, and the plant grows well in perennial borders or large rockeries. Propagation is usually by division when dormant, but raising from seed is also practical.

Species, variety or cultivar:
–
Other common names:
Bear's Foot, Lady's Mantle, Lion's Foot
Height and spread:
50 x 80 cm (30 x 32 in)
Blooming period:
Summer
Soil type:
Moist, well-drained soil
Sun or Shade:
Enjoys both full and part-sun
Hardiness:
Minimum temp –34°C (–30°F)

Allium cristophii • *Star of Persia*

DESCRIPTION

A genus of around 700 species of bulbous perennials and biennials in the onion (Alliaceae) family. The foliage may be fine and grassy, strappy or hollow and tubular, and the flowers, often brightly coloured, are most often borne in rounded heads atop long stems.

A. *cristophii* is found in central Asia and parts of Iran and Turkey, and has narrow to broad blue-green leaves to 40 cm (16 in) long, with downy undersides, two to seven per bulb. A strong-ribbed flower stem supports a 10–20 cm (4–8 in) wide rounded head of small, starry, metallic purple flowers.

Species, variety or cultivar:
  –
Other common names:
  Star of Persia
Height and spread:
  50 x 30 cm (20 x 12 in)
Blooming period:
  Summer
Soil type:
  Light, well-drained soil
Sun or Shade:
  Prefers full sun
Hardiness:
  Minimum temp −18°C (0°F)

Alocasia x amazonica • *White Alder*

DESCRIPTION

Comprising 70 species, this genus occurs in a variety of habitats, from lowland rainforests to swamps, roadsides and mountain regions from tropical southern Asia, Indonesia, Malaysia, New Guinea, Australia, to islands of the Pacific.

A. x amazonica is a hybrid of *A. lowii* and *A. sanderiana*, and its origins are unknown. The leaves are up to 60 cm (24 in) long and 30 cm (12 in) wide, and are arrowhead-shaped, the upperside being dark green, with a yellow-greenish white midrib, other veins silvery white. The underside is a dull purple, with green-white major veins, and the 45 cm (18 in) long leaf stalk is green.

Species, variety or cultivar:
  –
Other common names:
  White Alder
Height and spread:
  150 x 100 cm (60 x 40 in)
Blooming period:
  Summer
Soil type:
  Moist soil
Sun or Shade:
  Needs shade
Hardiness:
  Minimum temp 4°C (40°F)

Alstroemeria ligtu • *St Martin's Flower*

DESCRIPTION

A genus of around 50 species of fleshy-rooted perennials and the type genus for its family, the Alstroemeriaceae. Found in South America, often at altitude, they are known for their long-lasting beautifully marked flowers but notorious for their vigorous roots and self-sowing. At least one species, *A. psitticana*, is considered a weed in some areas.

A. *ligtu* is a summer-flowering species from Chile and Argentina, with leaves to 8 cm (3 in) long. White through creamy yellow, and lavender to magenta flowers with yellow throat and darker flecks. Flowers in clusters of two to three blooms in heads of up to eight clusters.

Species, variety or cultivar:
–
Other common names:
St Martin's Flower
Height and spread:
60 x 40 cm (24 x 16 in)
Blooming period:
Summer
Soil type:
Moderately fertile, well-drained soil
Sun or Shade:
Likes full sun
Hardiness:
Minimum temp –12°C (10°F)

Alstroemeria • *Lily of the Incas*

DESCRIPTION

There are about 50 species of fleshy-rooted perennials in this South American genus. The foliage is mid-green, usually lance-shaped and slightly twisted. It is carried on tall stems that terminate in many flowered heads of 6-petalled lily-like blooms that occur in many shades.

Alstroemerias hybridize freely, and in recent years the range has increased enormously as plant breeders have capitalized on these easily grown plants. They are ideal to use as cut flowers. Many are hybrids between *A. ligtu*, *A. haemantha*, and *A. aurea*. One popular hybrid is 'Apollo', which is 0.9 m (3 ft) tall, with white flowers and a brown-flecked deep yellow centre.

Species, variety or cultivar:
hybrid cultivar, 'Apollo'

Other common names:
Lily of the Incas, Peruvian Lily

Height and spread:
90 x 60 cm (36 x 24 in)

Blooming period:
Summer

Soil type:
Moderately fertile, well-drained soil, kept moist during the flowering season

Sun or Shade:
Likes full sun

Hardiness:
Minimum temp −18°C (0°F)

Alstroemeria • *Lily of the Incas*

DESCRIPTION

Originally from South America, this genus of about 50 species of fleshy-rooted perennials was named by Linnaeus after one of his pupils, Claus von Alstroemer (1736–1794), who around 1753 sent seeds of the plant to Linnaeus from Spain, where it had recently been introduced.

In recent years the range of *Alstroemeria* hybrids has greatly increased, (most being hybrids between *A. ligtu*, *A. haemantha* and *A. aurea*), as flower breeders have capitalized on the popularity of these easily grown plants for the cut flower market. 'Orange Glory' is a 0.9 m (3 ft) tall hybrid, which has dark-marked deep orange flowers with golden throats.

Species, variety or cultivar:
hybrid cultivar, 'Orange Glory'
Other common names:
Lily of the Incas, Peruvian Lily
Height and spread:
75 x 60 cm (30 x 24 in)
Blooming period:
Summer
Soil type:
Moderately fertile, well-drained soil, kept moist during the flowering season
Sun or Shade:
Likes full sun
Hardiness:
Minimum temp –18°C (0°F)

Amaryllis belladonna • *Belladonna Lily*

DESCRIPTION

This once large genus has now been reduced to just one species, an autumn-flowering bulb native to South Africa's Cape region.

It is the type genus for its family, the Amaryllidaceae. Dormant for most of the warmer months, sturdy red-tinted flower stems begin to appear from late summer and grow quickly to as much as 60 cm (24 in) tall. They are topped with mildly scented, funnel-shaped, 10 cm (4 in) long flowers in heads of six or more, in shades from very pale pink to deep magenta.

Belladonna means 'beautiful lady' and is a reference to the legend of Amaryllis, a beautiful shepherdess who appeared in the works of Virgil.

Species, variety or cultivar:
–

Other common names:
Belladonna Lily, Jersey Lily, March Lily, Naked Ladies

Height and spread:
60 x 50 cm (24 x 20 in)

Blooming period:
Summer

Soil type:
Well-drained soil

Sun or Shade:
Prefers a warm sunny position

Hardiness:
Minimum temp –12°C (10°F)

Anaphalis triplinervis • *Pearly Everlasting*

DESCRIPTION

This genus consists of around 100 species of perennials that may be upright, low and bushy or trailing. The leaves attach directly to the stems without a leaf stalk, and a feature common to all is that the foliage and stems are covered with a fine white to grey hair. The flowers last well when cut but are not that attractive, the plants being grown as much for their foliage.

A. *triplinervis* is a Central Asian species with spatula-shaped grey-green leaves to 10 cm (4 in) long and dome-shaped heads of white flowers in summer. 'Sommerschnee' grows to 75 cm (30 in) tall and has bright silvery white flowers.

Species, variety or cultivar:
  'Sommerschnee'
Other common names:
  Pearly Everlasting
Height and spread:
  75 x 50 cm (30 x 20 in)
Blooming period:
  Summer
Soil type:
  Gritty, well-drained soil, kept moist in summer
Sun or Shade:
  Likes full sun
Hardiness:
  Minimum temp −29°C (−20°F)

Anemone coronaria • *Wind Poppy*

DESCRIPTION

A. coronaria is a tuberous-rooted native of southeastern Europe and the northern Mediterranean, with finely divided ferny base foliage and simple leaves on flower stems. Large flowers in most shades except yellow are borne in spring. This species is the parent of many cultivars and a large range of garden hybrids, such as the Mona Lisa Series, which grow to 60 cm (24 in) tall with flowers to 10 cm (4 in) wide in all colours. The name Anemone is derived most likely from the Greek *anemos* (wind), though some consider it to come from *Naamen*, a variation on Adonis. Legend says it was his blood that gave *A. coronaria* its red flowers.

Species, variety or cultivar:
Mona Lisa Series

Other common names:
Florist's Anemone, Wind Poppy, Windflower

Height and spread:
60 x 40 cm (24 x 16 in)

Blooming period:
Spring

Soil type:
Moist, well-drained soil

Sun or Shade:
Likes both full sun and dappled shade

Hardiness:
Minimum temp –12°C (10°F)

Anemone hupehensis • *Windflower*

DESCRIPTION

Widespread in temperate regions of both hemispheres, this buttercup (Ranunculaceae) family genus encompasses some 120 species of perennials. Most species flower in spring shortly after the foliage appears, but some continue into early summer and a few bloom in autumn, such as *A. hupehensis*, which is a fibrous-rooted, late summer- to autumn-flowering species from China and Japan. This species has coarsely toothed, lightly downy, 3-part foliage and upright branching flower stems with large flowers, usually white but often in pink shades, and fluffy seedheads that follow. *A. h. var. japonica* has stocky flower stems and many-petalled flowers.

Species, variety or cultivar:
var. japonica
Other common names:
Windflower
Height and spread:
90 x 100 cm (36 x 40 in)
Blooming period:
Spring to autumn
Soil type:
Moist, well-drained soil
Sun or Shade:
Enjoys both full sun and part-shade
Hardiness:
Minimum temp –23°C (–10°F)

Anemone sylvestris • *Snowdrop Anemone*

DESCRIPTION

The roughly 120 perennial species of this genus are widespread in temperate regions of both hemispheres, and belong to the buttercup (Ranunculaceae) family. Their roots may be tuberous, fleshy-stemmed or fibrous, and develop into clumps of finely divided foliage. The bowl-shaped flowers, solitary or in small clusters, are borne on wiry stems well above the foliage.

A. *sylvestris* is a spreading fleshy-stemmed European species occurring in a range of conditions from lowland woods to subalpine. With deeply divided, deep green, hand-shaped leaves the species has, from late spring, scented white flowers up to 8 cm (3 in) wide, often slightly drooping, followed by fluffy seedheads.

Species, variety or cultivar:
–
Other common names:
Snowdrop Anemone, Snowdrop Windflower
Height and spread:
30 x 50 cm (12 x 20 in)
Blooming period:
Spring
Soil type:
Moist, well-drained soil
Sun or Shade:
Likes both full sun and part-sun
Hardiness:
Minimum temp –34°C (–30°F)

Anthemis tinctoria • *Dyer's Chamomile*

DESCRIPTION

Although this genus, along with many others in the daisy (Asteraceae) family, has been revised, it still contains around 100 species. *A. tinctoria* is a shrubby perennial found from Europe to western Asia, with short, finely divided leaves, usually light green and faintly hairy, sometimes downy. Masses of small yellow flowers appear throughout the warmer months. The flowers of *A. tinctoria* were once used to make dye and some species are being investigated for the medicinal properties of their essential oils and other extracts. 'Golden Rays' is an attractive cultivar, 60 cm (24 in) tall, with bright golden yellow flowers.

Species, variety or cultivar:
  'Golden Rays'
Other common names:
  Dyer's Chamomile, Yellow Chamomile
Height and spread:
  60 x 100 cm (24 x 40 in)
Blooming period:
  Summer
Soil type:
  Moist, fertile, well-drained soil
Sun or Shade:
  Prefers full sun
Hardiness:
  Minimum temp –23°C (–10°F)

Anthemis tinctoria • *Dyer's Chamomile*

DESCRIPTION

There are roughly 100 species in this genus of aromatic perennials and small shrubs, with leaves that are usually very finely divided, sometimes grey-green or silvery, and which form a base foliage clump with the yellow or white, rarely mauve, daisy flowers held above the foliage.

A. *tinctoria*, a shrubby perennial found from Europe to western Asia, has leaves which are usually light green and faintly hairy, sometimes downy, short and finely divided. An abundance of small flowers appear from late spring through summer. The cultivar 'Wargrave Variety' (*syn.* 'Wargrave'), has stems to 0.9 m (3 ft) tall with dark green leaves and lemon yellow flowers.

Species, variety or cultivar:
'Wargrave Variety'
Other common names:
Dyer's Chamomile, Yellow Chamomile
Height and spread:
90 x 100 cm (36 x 40 in)
Blooming period:
Summer
Soil type:
Moist, fertile, well-drained soil
Sun or Shade:
Prefers full sun
Hardiness:
Minimum temp –23°C (–10°F)

Anthurium andraeanum • *Flamingo Flower*

DESCRIPTION

Widely grown as houseplants but also grown outdoors in the tropics, this genus from tropical America encompasses around 900 species of evergreen perennials. *A. andraeanum* is from Colombia and Ecuador and has dark green arrowhead-shaped leaves up to 50 cm (20 in) long on equally long stalks. Bright, deep red, glossy, heavily veined, heart-shaped spathes to 15 cm (6 in) long, with white to cream spadix and red fruit, are borne year-round in ideal conditions.

Anthuriums last well as cut flowers and are an important industry in Hawaii, where at the peak of production in the 1980s around 30 million flower stems were shipped to the world's markets.

Species, variety or cultivar:
–
Other common names:
Flamingo Flower
Height and spread:
120 x 60 cm (48 x 24 in)
Blooming period:
All year
Soil type:
Moist, humus-rich soil
Sun or Shade:
Prefers half sun to full shade
Hardiness:
Minimum temp 4°C (40°F)

Antigonon leptopus • *Chain of Love*

DESCRIPTION

A Mexican and Central American genus comprising three species of quick-growing perennial vines that form dense canopies of usually heart-shaped foliage, smothered throughout the warmer months in floral racemes that derive most of their colour, usually bright pink, from the sepals that surround the tiny flowers.

A. leptopus is a strong-growing tuberous-rooted Mexican climber that will cover almost any support. The foliage is pointed, heavily veined, elongated, with heart-shaped leaves, strongly frilled margins and minute flowers enclosed by coral pink to red heart-shaped sepals. Frequent feeding encourages strong growth and heavy flowering. Pinch back to keep the plant compact and remove spent flowers to prolong blooming.

Species, variety or cultivar:
–

Other common names:
Chain of Love, Confederate Vine, Coral Vine, Mexican Creeper

Height and spread:
4.5 x 6 m (15 x 20 ft)

Blooming period:
Summer

Soil type:
Well-drained soil

Sun or Shade:
Prefers full sun

Hardiness:
Minimum temp –1°C (30°F)

Aquilegia vulgaris • *Columbine*

DESCRIPTION

This buttercup (Ranunculaceae) family genus is made up of about 70 species found over much of the temperate and subarctic Northern Hemisphere. Various species were used medicinally by Native North Americans.

A. *vulgaris* is found over much of Europe and has ferny foliage and flowers in white and shades of blue, mauve and red, including double-flowered forms, but the true species is seldom seen. The Flore Pleno Group has rich purple double flowers and there are many cultivars, such as 'Graeme Iddon', a tall cultivar with white flowers, which has spawned a range of double-flowered forms.

Species, variety or cultivar:
Flore Pleno Group, 'Graeme Iddon Red and White'

Other common names:
Columbine, Granny's Bonnet

Height and spread:
90 x 45 cm (36 x 18 in)

Blooming period:
Spring to summer

Soil type:
Cool, moist, humus-rich, well-drained soil

Sun or Shade:
Likes half sun, but can cope with full sun

Hardiness:
Minimum temp –40°C (–40°F)

Arabis alpina • *Rock Cress*

DESCRIPTION

There are about 120 species of annuals and perennials in this genus, mainly from Eurasia and western North America, but also other northern temperate zones. Their leaves are simple, sometimes downy or grey-green, and are often borne in tufted rosettes. In spring and early summer they carry upright sprays of small 4-petalled flowers, usually white or purple.

A. *alpina* is a small, slowly spreading perennial from the mountains of Europe, with simple leaves made slightly silver by fine hairs, and downy racemes of white flowers, very occasionally pale pink. A. *a. subsp. caucasica* 'Schneehaube' (syn. A. *caucasica* 'Snowcap') is low and spreading with white flowers.

Species, variety or cultivar:
  subsp. caucasica
  'Schneehaube'
Other common names:
  Rock Cress
Height and spread:
  30 x 50 cm (12 x 20 in)
Blooming period:
  Spring
Soil type:
  Well-drained soil that remains
  moist in summer
Sun or Shade:
  Likes full sun to half sun
Hardiness:
  Minimum temp −29°C (−20°F)

Arabis x arendsii • *Rock Cress*

DESCRIPTION

A cabbage (Brassicaceae) family genus of
around 120 species, mainly evergreen and
sometimes woody-stemmed. Widespread in the
northern temperate zones, especially Eurasia
and western North America, they tend to be
small plants that are often most at home in
rock crevices.

A. *x arendsii* is a garden hybrid between *A.
aubrietoides* and *A. caucasica*, usually low and
spreading, and forming tufted foliage clumps.
Flower stems grow to 15 cm (6 in) high, with
deep pink flowers. Several selections have
been made, including 'Compinkie' (syn. *A.
caucasica* 'Compinkie'), a neat compact plant
with bright pink flowers.

Species, variety or cultivar:
  'Compinkie'
Other common names:
  Rock Cress
Height and spread:
  20 x 60 cm (8 x 24 in)
Blooming period:
  Spring
Soil type:
  Well-drained soil that remains
  moist in summer
Sun or Shade:
  Enjoys both full and half-sun
Hardiness:
  Minimum temp –29°C (–20°F)

Arenaria montana • *Sandwort*

DESCRIPTION

This genus of about 160 low-growing, largely perennial, woody herbs and some annuals from the Caryophyllaceae family grows naturally across the temperate Northern Hemisphere. They are ideal as rock-garden plants and compact ground covers. Their shallow root system can make them drought sensitive. The genus derives its name from the Latin for sand, arena, referring to a preference for sandy soils.

A. *montana* is a robust prostrate perennial species from southwestern Europe, with loose mats of narrow, grey-green, hairy leaves and white flowers, 15–18 mm across, solitary or in few-flowered cymes, from spring–early summer. 'Avalanche,' bears more profuse, larger white flowers.

Species, variety or cultivar:
–
Other common names:
Sandwort
Height and spread:
15 x 60 cm (6 x 24 in)
Blooming period:
Spring to summer
Soil type:
Will tolerate poor soils, but soil should be moist, sandy and well-drained
Sun or Shade:
Prefers partial shade
Hardiness:
Minimum temp –34°C (–30°F)

Argemone munita • *Prickly Poppy*

DESCRIPTION

A genus of 23 species in the poppy (Papaveraceae) family, occurring in North and South America, the West Indies and Hawaii. Erect stems are produced from fleshy roots, and

the leaves are smooth-edged or deeply lobed, prickly or smooth and bluish green.

A. *munita* is a multi-stemmed, herbaceous perennial, occurring in the chapparal and woodlands of several western States of the USA, and growing at altitudes from 800 m to 2,500 m, with deeply lobed, prickly and greyish leaves. White flowers, up to 8 cm (3 in) across, with crinkly petals, spiny sepals, and up to 250 yellow stamens per flower bloom in summer.

Species, variety or cultivar:
–
Other common names:
Prickly Poppy
Height and spread:
90 x 50 cm (36 x 20 in)
Blooming period:
Summer to autumn
Soil type:
Well-draining, gravelly soils
Sun or Shade:
Needs full sun
Hardiness:
Minimum temp −18°C (0°F)

Argyranthemum

DESCRIPTION

From the Canary Islands and Madeira, the 24 members of this genus belong to the daisy (Asteraceae) family. Popular in gardens and as cut flowers there are numerous cultivars, most with 'double' or 'semi-double' flowerheads, appearing over a long season. Leaves have a slightly aromatic, bitter smell when bruised. The long-stalked flowerheads are borne in loose groups of two to five blooms.

Although many references have included all Argyranthemum cultivars under the species *A. frutescens*, it seems clear that most present-day cultivars are of hybrid origin. Apart from *A. frutescens*, likely parent species include *A. foeniculaceum* and *A. maderense*. The hybrid cultivar 'Petite Pink' has attractive single pink flowers.

Species, variety or cultivar:
  hybrid cultivar, 'Petite Pink'
Other common names:
  —
Height and spread:
  75 x 90 cm (30 x 36 in)
Blooming period:
  Spring to summer
Soil type:
  Very well-drained soil, not too rich
Sun or Shade:
  Likes full sun or part-sun
Hardiness:
  Minimum temp –7°C (20°F)

Armeria juniperifolia • *Sea Pink*

DESCRIPTION

Armeria was the Roman name for Dianthus and was given to this genus because of a supposed resemblance, also reflected in the common name, sea pink. However, Armeria comes from a different family, the leadworts (Plumbaginaceae), and not the pink family. The genus comprises around 80 species of herbaceous and shrubby perennials found in Eurasia, North Africa and the American Pacific coast. The plants occur in a wide range of environments and are easily cultivated, being especially at home in rockeries. Most are hardy and prefer moist well-drained soil and a position in full or half-sun. Propagate from seed or cuttings, or by the careful division of well-established clumps.

A. juniperifolia is a small shrubby species native to Spain, with very short, fine hairy, aromatic, grassy leaves. The flower stems less than 5 cm (2 in) long, and pink to magenta flowerheads, 12 mm (½ in) wide appear from spring through summer.

ABOVE: Armeria juniperia is one of the best species for the rock garden. This alpine thrift comes from central Spain, where it grows in mountain pastures and rock crevices. It likes a sharply drained soil and a sunny site.

Species, variety or cultivar:
–
Other common names:
Sea Pink, Thrift
Height and spread:
15 x 20 cm (6 x 8 in)
Blooming period:
Spring to summer
Soil type:
Moist, well-drained soil
Sun or Shade:
Enjoys full or half-sun
Hardiness:
Minimum temp –12°C (10°F)

Armeria maritima • *Sea Pink*

DESCRIPTION

The roughly 80 species of herbaceous and shrubby perennials in this genus are found in Eurasia, North Africa and the American Pacific coast. They form clumps of simple linear leaves, above which rounded heads of tiny flowers with colourful bracts are held in spring and summer. The name 'thrift' is applied in the sense of the meaning 'to thrive,' because the plant grows under harsh conditions. They are easily cultivated, and occur in a variety of environments, but they particularly love rockeries. Most are hardy and prefer moist, well-drained soil and a position in full or half-sun.

A. *maritima* is a mounding perennial or subshrub found across the northern temperate zone, with grassy deep green leaves to 10 cm (4 in) long. Flower stems to 30 cm (12 in) tall with 25 mm (1 in) wide heads of white, pink or red flowers occur from spring through summer.

BELOW: Armeria maritima has distinctive 5-petal open flowers.

Species, variety or cultivar:
  —
Other common names:
  Sea Pink, Thrift
Height and spread:
  30 x 40 cm (12 x 16 in)
Blooming period:
  Spring to summer
Soil type:
  Moist, well-drained soil
Sun or Shade:
  Likes full or half-sun
Hardiness:
  Minimum temp –34°C (–30°F)

Artemisia

DESCRIPTION

This genus of about 300 species of evergreen herbs and shrubs is spread throughout northern temperate regions with some also found in southern Africa and South America. The beauty of these plants lies in their attractive foliage which is well dissected and of palest grey to silver. The plants are frequently aromatic. Tarragon, the popular culinary herb, is a member of this genus.

A. 'Powis Castle' is possibly a hybrid between *A. arborescens* and the herbaceous *A. pontica*. It is similar to *A. arborescens*, but its habit is more sprawling, with woody stems usually lying on the ground, and its foliage is a striking silvery grey-green.

Species, variety or cultivar:
  hybrid cultivar, 'Powis Castle'
Other common names:
  –
Height and spread:
  0.6 x 1.2 m (2 x 4 ft)
Blooming period:
  Summer
Soil type:
  Well-drained soil
Sun or Shade:
  Prefers full sun
Hardiness:
  Minimum temp −18°C (0°F)

Arum alpinum

DESCRIPTION

A genus of about 26 species of tuberous-rooted perennials commonly known as lilies but actually of the family Araceae, found from western Europe to the Himalayas and centred around the Mediterranean. The somewhat unpleasant scent and dark purple-red colouration of many arums mimics rotting flesh and attracts pollinating flies – unpleasant but effective.

A. alpinum is a native of Europe, from Sweden to Spain and Crete, with arrowhead-shaped leaves that usually die away from autumn, though not always completely in mild climates. A pale green spadix is enclosed in a 12 cm (5 in) green spathe, purple-tinted within. Flowers appear in early summer and clustered berries follow.

Species, variety or cultivar:
ssp. danicum
Other common names:
–
Height and spread:
30 x 40 cm (12 x 16 in)
Blooming period:
Spring to summer
Soil type:
Cool, humus-rich soil that remains moist over summer
Sun or Shade:
Prefers half-sun
Hardiness:
Minimum temp –12°C (10°F)

Asclepias tuberosa • *Butterfly Weed*

DESCRIPTION

This American and African genus comprises over 100 species and includes annuals, perennials, subshrubs and shrubs among its number. All parts of the plants exude a milky sap if cut, hence the common name, milkweed. Easily grown in any light, well-drained soil in full sun, milkweeds will, however, have more luxuriant foliage and will flower more heavily if well-fed and watered. They grow readily and quickly from seed, and can be treated as annuals or short-lived perennials. Trim to shape, not into bare wood, as plants can be very slow to recover from harsh pruning.

A. tuberosa is a woody-based perennial herb native to eastern and southern USA. The species has narrow lance-shaped leaves, spiralling on crowded stems and heads (cymes) of small 5-petalled yellow, orange or vermilion flowers. The flowers are followed by inflated seed pods, sometimes unusually shaped, that are tightly packed with small seeds, each with a small parachute of silky down.

ABOVE: The seed pods of asclepias are valued in dried flower arrangements. They have a long bloom period from late spring throughout the summer. Their flowers are a nectar source for many butterflies and their leaves are a food source for monarch butterfly larvae (caterpillars). Also commonly called pleurisy root in reference to a prior medicinal use of the plant roots to treat lung inflammations.

Species, variety or cultivar:
–

Other common names:
Butterfly Weed, Pleurisy Root, Milkweed

Height and spread:
90 x 30 cm (36 x 12 in)

Blooming period:
Summer

Soil type:
Light, well-drained soil

Sun or Shade:
Prefers full sun

Hardiness:
Minimum temp –40°C (–40°F)

Asphodeline lutea • *Jacob's Rod*

DESCRIPTION

This genus is a member of the lily (Liliaceae) family and has 18 to 20 species of fleshy-stemmed perennial or biennial herbs native to southern Europe where they grow on rocky slopes and in scrubby areas. They are clump-forming plants with greyish green linear leaves to 30 cm (12 in) long, sometimes with slightly serrated margins. The flowers are borne in spring and summer, have six flaring petals, yellow or white tinged with pink, and are scented in some species.

A. lutea is from the Mediterranean, with narrow silvery leaves to 30 cm (12 in) long, and fragrant yellow flowers, borne on stiff spikes, from late spring–summer.

Species, variety or cultivar:

–

Other common names:
Jacob's Rod, King's Spear, Yellow Asphodel

Height and spread:
120 x 30 cm (48 x 12 in)

Blooming period:
Spring to summer

Soil type:
Moderately fertile soil

Sun or Shade:
Likes full sun

Hardiness:
Minimum temp –18°C (0°F)

Aster x frikartii • *Michaelmas Daisy*

DESCRIPTION

Found across the temperate Northern
Hemisphere and into South America, this group
of 250 species of mainly herbaceous perennials
is the type genus for the daisy (Asteraceae)
family. Upright plants that often sprawl under
the weight of their foliage and flowers, they
usually have simple linear to lance-shaped
leaves, sometimes hairy and/or serrated edges.

A. x frikartii is a garden hybrid between *A.
amellus* and *A. thomsonii*. An upright perennial
with dark green, elongated, lance-shaped base
leaves, it has branching sprays of 5 cm (2 in)
wide daisies in shades of lavender and purple-
blue in autumn. The cultivar 'Mönch' bears
attractive mauve-purple flowers.

Species, variety or cultivar:
  'Mönch'
Other common names:
  Michaelmas Daisy
Height and spread:
  40 x 40 cm (16 x 16 in)
Blooming period:
  Autumn
Soil type:
  Well-drained soil that stays
  damp in the growing season
Sun or Shade:
  Enjoys both full and part-sun
Hardiness:
  Minimum temp –34°C (–30°F)

Aster radula • *Michaelmas Daisy*

DESCRIPTION

There are 250 species of mainly herbaceous perennials in this genus found across the temperate Northern Hemisphere and into South America. A few flower in spring but most bloom in late summer and autumn, producing large heads of small to medium-sized daisies in a range of colours. Asters feature in ancient myths, the ancient Greeks believing that they repelled snakes and were an antidote to their venom.

A. *radula* is an upright summer-flowering perennial from western Canada, which has angular stems with pointed elliptical leaves to 10 cm (4 in) long, sometimes toothed, with downy undersides. The flowerheads, solitary or in small sprays, are violet.

Species, variety or cultivar:
–
Other common names:
Michaelmas Daisy
Height and spread:
1.2 x 0.8 m (48 x 32 in)
Blooming period:
Summer
Soil type:
Well-drained soil that stays damp in the growing season
Sun or Shade:
Likes full and part-sun
Hardiness:
Minimum temp −29°C (−20°F)

Astilbe chinensis • *False Spiraea*

OF DESCRIPTION

Found mainly in temperate East Asia, this perennial genus of the saxifrage (Saxifragaceae) family includes just 12 species but has been extensively selected and hybridized to produce a myriad garden plants. Their toothed pinnate leaves sprout directly from fleshy stems and soon form a large foliage clump.

A. chinensis is native to China and Japan, and has foliage with large and coarsely toothed leaflets. The flowerheads are short-stemmed with strongly upright plumes, and there are several natural varieties, including *A. c.* 'Visions', a typically compact cultivar with 45 cm (18 in) tall, honey-scented, red flower sprays and bronze foliage.

Species, variety or cultivar:
  'Visions'
Other common names:
  False Spiraea
Height and spread:
  70 x 50 cm (27 x 20 in)
Blooming period:
  Summer
Soil type:
  Moist, humus-rich,
  woodland soil
Sun or Shade:
  Likes dappled sun
Hardiness:
  Minimum temp –29°C
  (–20°F)

Astilbe • *False Spiraea*

DESCRIPTION

Although we think of astilbe plumes as being bright and showy, the name actually means without brilliance, coming from the Greek, meaning 'without' and stilbe meaning 'brilliance'. That is because although the flowerheads are bright, each flower is, on its

own, tiny and rather dull. Astilbes are not drought tolerant and prefer dappled sunlight. They often thrive around pond margins but do tolerate being waterlogged.

The numerous hybrid cultivars have *A. japonica* as a major part of their heritage, and include 'Red Sentinel', which grows to 60–90 cm (24–36 in) high, and has bronze leaves and open sprays of red flowers on red stems.

Species, variety or cultivar:
   hybrid cultivar, 'Red Sentinel'
Other common names:
   False Spiraea
Height and spread:
   90 x 90 cm (36 x 36 in)
Blooming period:
   Summer
Soil type:
   Moist, humus-rich, woodland
   soil
Sun or Shade:
   Enjoys dappled sun
Hardiness:
   Minimum temp –23°C
   (–10°F)

Aubrieta • *Aubretia*

DESCRIPTION

Found from Europe to Central Asia, the 12 evergreen cushion or mat-forming perennials of this genus are members of the cabbage (Brassicaceae) family. Indispensable for rockeries and also a colourful addition to flower borders or spilling over banks, they smother themselves in flowers in spring and early summer, becoming carpets of tiny, 4-petalled, purple, mauve or white blooms. The foliage is small and simple, usually dull grey-green and finely downy, often with small lobes or teeth.

Garden hybrids probably all have *A. deltoidea* in their background. All are mat-forming, but otherwise highly variable. 'Doctor Mules,' has a neat, compact habit with attractive mauve-blue flowers.

Species, variety or cultivar:
  hybrid cultivar, 'Doctor Mules'
Other common names:
  Aubretia
Height and spread:
  15 x 60 cm (6 x 24 in)
Blooming period:
  Spring to early summer
Soil type:
  Gritty, well-drained soil
Sun or Shade:
  Full or half-sun
Hardiness:
  Minimum temp −18°C (0°F)

Baptisia australis • *Blue False Indigo*

DESCRIPTION

B. australis is commonly known as blue false indigo – a name acquired from its use in dyemaking, as a substitute for true indigo. This species is native to central and eastern USA, and is now threatened in some states. An upright or spreading bushy perennial, this plant has striking bluish green foliage. Blooming in summer, *B. australis* produces lupin-like spikes of purplish blue flowers. The flowers are followed by erect inflated seed pods, which can be dried for floral arrangements. Propagation is from seed or by division. If planting in an exposed position, it may be necessary to stake the plant when it becomes taller.

Species, variety or cultivar:
–
Other common names:
Blue False Indigo
Height and spread:
1.2 x 1.2 m (4 x 4 ft)
Blooming period:
Summer
Soil type:
Deep, well-drained soil that is neutral or slightly acidic
Sun or Shade:
Enjoys full sun to part-sun
Hardiness:
Minimum temp –29°C (–20°F)

Belamcanda chinensis • *Leopard Lily*

DESCRIPTION

The genus Belamcanda belongs to the iris
(Iridaceae) family. *B. australis* is a short-lived
rhizomatous perennial found from eastern
Russia to Japan. It bears deciduous leaves
that are sword-like and arranged in fans.
Borne on loose spikes in summer, the flowers
have six narrow flaring petals and range
from yellow to orange, usually speckled in
shades of purple. Fruiting capsules that split
to reveal large black seeds follow the flowers.
These plants should be well watered during
the growing period, and in cooler climates
they will need an application of protective
mulch in winter. Propagate these plants from
seed, or division in spring or early autumn.

Species, variety or cultivar:
–
Other common names:
BlackberryLily, Leopard Lily
Height and spread:
90 x 30 cm (36 x 12 in)
Blooming period:
Summer
Soil type:
Well-drained, moderately fertile
soil
Sun or Shade:
Does best in full sun
Hardiness:
Minimum temp –12°C (10°F)

Bellis perennis • *Bellis Daisy*

DESCRIPTION

Native to Europe and the Mediterranean, the genus Bellis contains seven species of annual and perennial daisies including the common bellis daisy (*B. perennis*), which is the little white flower that pops up on many of the world's lawns. This familiar daisy features broad, spatula-shaped leaves and pink-tinted white flowers carried on individual stems. The leaves and extracts have been used in herbal medicines to treat wounds and for their anti-inflammatory properties. The genus name is derived from the Latin *bellus*, meaning pretty, and although the wild species are sometimes weeds, the cultivated forms are indeed attractive. The fancy cultivars are propagated by division, others from seed.

Species, variety or cultivar:
–
Other common names:
Bellis daisy
Height and spread:
10 x 20 cm (4 x 8 in)
Blooming period:
Late winter
Soil type:
Moist soil
Sun or Shade:
Does best in part-sun
Hardiness:
Minimum temp –34°C (–30°F)

Bergenia cordifolia • *Heartleaf Saxifrage*

DESCRIPTION

A temperate-climate genus, Bergenia is named for an eighteenth-century German botanist, Karl August von Bergen, while it acquired its common name of pigsqueak from the sound made by rubbing the wet leaves between one's fingers. The species *B. cordifolia* is native to the mountains of Siberia and Mongolia. The rounded toothed-edged leaves, which can reach up to 20 cm (8 in) long, are produced on tough, woody, fleshy stalks. From late winter, 5-petalled bright pink flowers are borne on long red stems from late winter. There are a number of cultivars available, including 'Perfecta', which bears its brilliant pink flowers on very tall flower stems, complemented by red-tinted foliage.

Species, variety or cultivar:
'Perfecta'

Other common names:
Heartleaf saxifrage,
Pigsqueak

Height and spread:
40 x 120 cm
(16 x 48 in)

Blooming period:
Late winter

Soil type:
Humus-rich soil

Sun or Shade:
Does best in part-shade

Hardiness:
Minimum temp –40°C
(–40°F)

Bomarea caldasii • *Climbing Alstroemeria*

DESCRIPTION

The 100-odd tuberous-rooted perennials in this South American genus belong in the alstroemeria (Alstroemeriaceae) family and many of them climb, usually by twining. Most species have elongated, lance-shaped, 10–15 cm (4–6 in) long leaves on wiry stems that grow very quickly. Although nominally evergreen, the tops are frost tender and in all but the mildest temperate regions they will die down or become untidy over winter. However, provided the roots are well insulated with mulch, new shoots will appear in spring. Otherwise, lift the tubers for winter. Bomarea species can be propagated by division or from seed.

B. caldasii originates from northern South America. It produces simple or compound, pendulous, tubular to bell-shaped, open heads of 5 cm (2 in) long flowers. These spring-blooming flowers feature six tepals in two whorls – pinkish red to red-brown outer tepals, and yellow to orange inner tepals with brown, red or green spotting.

BELOW: The long-lasting flowers of *Bomarea caldasii* are carried in large ball-shaped clusters and are a rich orange usually during summer, but they have been known to flower at all different times of the year. Any soil in full light, hardy outdoors, but the roots do require some winter protection.

Species, variety or cultivar:
–

Other common names:
Climbing Alstroemeria

Height and spread:
5 x 1.8 m (17 x 6 ft)

Blooming period:
Late spring to autumn

Soil type:
Moist, humus-rich, well-drained soil

Sun or Shade:
Likes half-sun

Hardiness:
Minimum temp –7°C (20°F)

Brunnera macrophylla

DESCRIPTION

Closely related to the forget-me-nots and
resembling them in flower, the three species in
the Brunnera genus are fleshy-stemmed
herbaceous perennials belonging to the borage
(Boraginaceae) family. Named for Samuel
Brunner (1790–1844), a Swiss botanist, the
plants in this genus are found throughout
temperate Eurasia. The species often self-sow
and naturalize.

B. macrophylla is a native of Eastern Europe.
It bears fine hairy, broad, heart-shaped leaves,
each up to 15 cm (6 in) long, on 20 cm (8 in)
stalks. Sprays of soft blue flowers are held high
above the foliage on 50 cm (20 in) tall stalks.

Species, variety or cultivar:
   –
Other common names:
   –
Height and spread:
   50 x 80 cm (20 x 32 in)
Blooming period:
   Spring
Soil type:
   Moist, humus-rich, well-drained
   soil
Sun or Shade:
   Prefers part-shade
Hardiness:
   Minimum temp –40°C (–40°F)

Calluna vulgaris • *Heather*

DESCRIPTION

Native to northwestern Europe from Siberia to Turkey and Morocco, and the Azores, *C. vulgaris* is the sole species in this genus belonging to the erica (Ericaceae) family. The leaves grow in overlapping pairs, arranged oppositely, along the stems, and look more like scales. The species features dark green leaves, which usually turn reddish or purple-tinged in winter; leaves of the cultivars range from the palest yellow to grey-green, to dark bottle green. It produces racemes of tubular or bell-shaped, single or double, white or pink to purplish pink flowers from summer to late autumn. The cultivar 'Gold Haze', has attractive light golden foliage and white flowers.

Species, variety or cultivar:
'Gold Haze'

Other common names:
Heather, Ling

Height and spread:
60 x 75 cm (24 x 30 in)

Blooming period:
Summer to late autumn

Soil type:
Acid soil

Sun or Shade:
Sun or shade

Hardiness:
Minimum temp −34°C (−30°F)

Campanula carpatica • *Carpathian Bellflower*

DESCRIPTION

The genus Campanula contains about 300 species of hardy annual, biennial and perennial plants. They can be ground-hugging, clump-forming or erect and branching plants, and many are native to Mediterranean areas, the Balkans, and Caucasus region, while some are from North America and temperate Asia. A few species are invasive.

C. *carpatica*, from the Carpathian Mountains, is a low-growing perennial that forms a thick clump of small bright green leaves. In summer the plant is covered with pale blue or white, upward facing, open cup-shaped flowers, 2.5–5 cm (1–2 in) across. The cultivar 'Blaue Clips', produces attractive light blue flowers.

Species, variety or cultivar:
'Blaue Clips'

Other common names:
Carpathian Bellflower, Tussock bellflower

Height and spread:
40 x 30 cm (12 x 16 in)

Blooming period:
Summer

Soil type:
Reasonably well-drained, fertile soil

Sun or Shade:
Enjoys sun to half-sun

Hardiness:
Minimum temp –40°C (–40°F)

Campanula poscharskyana • *Serbian Bellflower*

DESCRIPTION

There are many popular and beautiful garden plants in the genus Campanula. They generally feature alternately arranged leaves, and blue, mauve, pale pink or white flowers. The flowers range from large drooping bells to delicate open stars, and are borne on panicles, spikes or singly. These plants can be propagated from seed, cuttings or by basal division.

Native to Croatia, *C. poscharskyana* is a vigorous alpine perennial. From summer to autumn, attractive starry flowers of lavender to violet are produced. This plant will spread rapidly if planted in the rock garden. The cultivar 'Multiplicity' bears double lavender-blue flowers.

Species, variety or cultivar:
'Multiplicity'
Other common names:
Serbian Bellflower
Height and spread:
20 x 60 cm (8 x 24 in)
Blooming period:
Summer to autumn
Soil type:
Reasonably fertile, well-drained soil
Sun or Shade:
Likes full sun to half-sun
Hardiness:
Minimum temp –23°C (–10°F)

Catananche caerulea • *Blue Cupidone*

DESCRIPTION

This small genus in the daisy (Asteraceae) family contains five species of annual or perennial herbs found in countries around the Mediterranean, although *C. caerulea* is usually the only species seen in cultivation. The leaves of most species are usually long and narrow and arise at the base of the clump. The thin wiry flowering stems bear cornflower-like flowers of blue, white or yellow.

Native to southwestern Europe and northern Africa, *C. caerulea* features low clumps of narrow lance-shaped greyish green leaves, sometimes with a few long teeth. Borne in summer, the blue cornflower-like flowers are held aloft on delicate stems.

Species, variety or cultivar:
–
Other common names:
Blue Cupidone, Blue
Succory, Cupid's Dart
Height and spread:
75 x 45 cm (30 x 18 in)
Blooming period:
Summer
Soil type:
Well-drained soil
Sun or Shade:
Prefers full sun
Hardiness:
Minimum temp –18°C
(0°F)

Centaurea dealbata • *Persian Cornflower*

DESCRIPTION

Widespread in the temperate zones, the genus
Centaurea encompasses around 450 species of
annuals, perennials and subshrubs. They are a
variable lot but most carry distinctive thistle-like
flowerheads, which come in a range of colours
including white, yellow, pink, mauve and blue.
The plants have an upright habit, and usually
feature pinnate foliage, which is often silver-grey.
Because some species have been used to treat
wounds, Centaurea was named after the Greek
mythological half-horse, half-man figure, the
Centaur, famed for his healing powers.

A caucasian and northern Iranian perennial,
C. dealbata has green pinnate leaves, with grey
furry undersides. The summer-borne flowers are
pink to purple.

Species, variety or cultivar:
–
Other common names:
Persian Cornflower
Height and spread:
100 x 60 cm (40 x 24 in)
Blooming period:
Summer
Soil type:
Light, well-drained soil
Sun or Shade:
Prefers full sun
Hardiness:
Minimum temp –40°C (–40°F)

Centaurea montana • *Mountain Bluet*

DESCRIPTION

With more than 400 members, the species of Centaurea are a variable lot. The flowerheads often have distinctly different inner and outer florets, with those on the outer having five narrow petals. The plants are prone to mildew, however, planting them in a spot with good ventilation will lessen any problems.

From the mountains of Europe, *C. montana* is a perennial species. It spreads by rhizomes and may form a large clump of broad, green, lance-shaped leaves that are sometimes pinnate at base. The summer-borne thistle-like flowers are violet to purple-blue. Propagate perennials by division or from softwood cuttings of non-flowering stems.

Species, variety or cultivar:
–
Other common names:
Mountain Bluet, Perennial Cornflower
Height and spread:
80 x 100 cm (32 x 40 in)
Blooming period:
Summer
Soil type:
Light, well-drained soil
Sun or Shade:
Prefers full sun
Hardiness:
Minimum temp –40°C (–40°F)

Centranthus ruber • *Jupiter's Beard*

DESCRIPTION

Centranthus consists of 12 species of annual and perennial subshrubs from Europe and the Mediterranean. Only one species, C. *ruber*, is widely cultivated, though it is inclined to self-sow, and is considered a weed in parts of New Zealand. As a rule, the species form clumps of upright stems with simple, lance-shaped, blue-green leaves and one topped with inflorescences of tiny flowers.

C. *ruber* is found in Europe, North Africa, and western Asia. It bears 8 cm (3 in) long, blue-green, oval to lance-shaped leaves, sometimes finely toothed. From late spring to late summer, it bears tiny, honey-scented, deep rose pink to red flowers massed in upright heads.

Species, variety or cultivar:
–

Other common names:
Jupiter's Beard, Red Valerian

Height and spread:
100 x 70 cm (40 x 27 in)

Blooming period:
Late spring to late summer

Soil type:
Alkaline soil

Sun or Shade:
Enjoys full sun to half-sun

Hardiness:
Minimum temp –23°C (–10°F)

Clematis x eriostemon • *Leather Vine*

DESCRIPTION

There are over 200 species in this genus in the buttercup (Ranunculaceae) family. They encompass a huge range of plants, which are mainly climbing or scrambling, but sometimes shrubby or perennial, deciduous or evergreen, flowering at any time in any colour, occurring in both northern and southern temperate zones and at higher altitudes in the tropics. Their leaves may be simple or pinnate and their flowers are nearly always showy, with four to eight petal-like sepals, which are followed by fluffy seedheads.

C. *x eriostemon* is probably a hybrid with C. *viticella*. It can reach up to 3 m (10 ft) tall, and bears large violet flowers.

Species, variety or cultivar:
–
Other common names:
Leather Vine, Traveller's Joy,
Virgin's Bower
Height and spread:
3 x 1.8 m (10 x 6 ft)
Blooming period:
Summer to autumn
Soil type:
Humus-rich soil
Sun or Shade:
Prefers full sun to half-sun
Hardiness:
Minimum temp –23°C (–10°F)

Clivia miniata • *Fire Lily*

Description

The genus Clivia is named not for Robert Clive of India fame/infamy but instead for his grand-daughter Lady Charlotte Clive, Duchess of Northumberland (died 1868). Belonging to the amaryllis (Amaryllidaceae), this genus is made up of four species of perennials from southern Africa.

C. *miniata* is a clump-forming perennial with long, bright green, strappy leaves that can reach up to 60 cm (24 in) long, and which are sometimes quite broad. Heads of wide open, funnel-shaped, yellow-throated, orange to nearly red flowers are produced in spring, and are followed by red berries. The cultivar 'Striata', has striking white or cream variegated foliage.

Species, variety or cultivar:
  'Striata'
Other common names:
  Fire Lily
Height and spread:
  60 x 100 cm (24 x 40 in)
Blooming period:
  Spring
Soil type:
  Loose, well-drained soil
Sun or Shade:
  Prefers part-shade
Hardiness:
  Minimum temp −7°C (20°F)

Convallaria majalis • *Lily-of-the-Valley*

DESCRIPTION

A traditional favourite, lily-of-the-valley has been cultivated since at least 1,000 BC. The sole species in the genus, *C. majalis*, is a low, spreading perennial that is found over much of the northern temperate zone. Its vigorous rhizomes can colonize a large area, producing bright green lance-shaped leaves and short-stemmed flowerheads from spring to early summer. The well-known, bell-shaped blooms are scented, waxy and usually white. The flowers are followed by red berries. When seventeenth-century herbalists recommended lily-of-the-valley to strengthen the heartbeat they were correct, because lily-of-the-valley contains glycoside compounds that have been used in modern heart medications.

Species, variety or cultivar:
  –
Other common names:
  Lily-of-the-Valley
Height and spread:
  20 x 100 cm (8 x 40 in)
Blooming period:
  Spring to early summer
Soil type:
  Deep, moist, well-drained soil
Sun or Shade:
  Does best in part-shade
Hardiness:
  Minimum temp –40°C (–40°F)

Convolvulus tricolor

Description

There are around 100 species of twiner climbers, soft-stemmed shrubs and herbaceous perennials in the genus Convolvulus, originating from many temperate regions.

  C. tricolor is an annual or short-lived perennial shrub or small climber, found through southern Europe and in North Africa. It bears small pointed oval leaves. The flowers, which can be up to 5 cm (2 in) wide, are borne singly in the leaf axils, in blue shades often with a yellow throat. The flowers usually appear in succession over a long period. Easily propagated from cuttings, the shrubby forms should be trimmed regularly to encourage density of growth.

Species, variety or cultivar:
  –
Other common names:
  –
Height and spread:
  100 x 80 cm (40 x 32 in)
Blooming period:
  Summer
Soil type:
  Adaptable to a range of soils
Sun or Shade:
  Likes full sun
Hardiness:
  Minimum temp –12°C (10°F)

Coreopsis • *Tickseed*

DESCRIPTION

Coreopsis species are found in the Americas, especially in the US southwest and Mexico. The 80-odd annuals and perennials in this genus, which is a member of the daisy (Asteraceae) family, are heavy-flowering, compact plants that are indispensable for summer colour. The flowers of the species are nearly always golden yellow, though garden forms occur in many shades. Both the common name of the genus – tickseed – and the meaning of the Greek word *coreopsis* (bug-like), from which the proper name is derived, refer to the appearance of the small black seeds.

Coreopsis 'Sunray' is a compact bushy plant with bright green smooth-edged and pinnate foliage. From late spring, it bears showy, glowing yellow, double flowers. This cheery garden addition flowers better with summer moisture but is quite drought tolerant. It may be raised from seed and will also grow from divisions or small basal cuttings of non-flowering stems.

Species, variety or cultivar:
  hybrid cultivar, 'Sunray'
Other common names:
  Tickseed
Height and spread:
  50 x 40 cm (20 x 16 in)
Blooming period:
  Late spring to summer
Soil type:
  Light well-drained soil
Sun or Shade:
  Does best in full sun
Hardiness:
  Minimum temp –18°C (0°F)

ABOVE: The vibrant, eye-catching, daisy-like, yellow blooms of Coreopsis make long-lasting cut flowers. They come in both single- and double-flowering varieties. Use these drought-tolerant plants in sunny, wild gardens, flower borders and containers. They attract songbirds. The common name comes from the shape of the seed, which is flattened like a tick.

Corydalis cheilanthifolia

DESCRIPTION

Many of the 300-odd species of annuals and perennials in this genus have long been cultivated. Mainly confined to the northern temperate zones, the perennial species spread by rhizomes or tubers to form clumps of ferny, often blue-green foliage. Although small, the flowers are usually very showy and combine well with the delicate foliage.

C. *cheilanthifolia* is native to central China. It forms loose rosettes of short-stemmed, ferny, olive green leaves, which can each measure up to 45 cm (18 in) long. Racemes of 12 mm (½ in) long bright yellow flowers are borne on stems to 45 cm (18 in) tall in spring.

Species, variety or cultivar:
–
Other common names:
–
Height and spread:
25 x 100 cm (10 x 40 in)
Blooming period:
Spring
Soil type:
Moist, cool, humus-rich soil
Sun or Shade:
Prefers part-shade
Hardiness:
Minimum temp –23°C (–10°F)

Crocosmia masoniorum • *Montbretia*

DESCRIPTION

Crocosmias come from the grasslands of South Africa and are valued for their handsome appearance, trouble-free lifestyles, bright flowers and erect lance-like leaves. The plants are fully dormant in winter. The corms are disc-like, ivory white and about 6 cm (2½ in) in diameter. Divide the corms regularly to combat overcrowding.

A robust plant from a mountainous habitat, *C. masoniorum* does best in mild climates and on moist sandy soils. The dense clumps of pleated mid-green leaves are a wonderful foil for the single, spraying, arching stems of funnel-shaped red-orange flowers. The cultivar 'Rowallane Yellow' features yellow flowers.

Species, variety or cultivar:
'Rowallane Yellow'
Other common names:
Falling Stars, Montbretia
Height and spread:
120 x 100 cm (48 x 40 in)
Blooming period:
Mid- to late summer
Soil type:
Rich, well-drained soil
Sun or Shade:
Does best in full sun
Hardiness:
Minimum temp −18°C (0°F)

Daboecia cantabrica • *St Dabeoc's Heath*

DESCRIPTION

The sole species in this genus, *D. cantabrica* (syn. *D. polifolia*) has a variable habitat and can be erect to very prostrate and straggling. Native to western Europe, its habitat covers heathland from coastal cliffs to mountains. The roughly egg-shaped leaves are shiny, dark green on the upper surface and silvery underneath. The small, urn-shaped, pale to pinkish violet flowers, carried in racemes clear of the foliage, appear from mid-summer to mid-autumn. Cut back after flowering. There are several subspecies and a number of cultivars. Propagate by sowing seeds in spring or take half-hardened cuttings, especially of cultivars, in summer.

Species, variety or cultivar:
–
Other common names:
St Dabeoc's Heath
Height and spread:
38 x 65 cm (15 x 26 in)
Blooming period:
Mid-summer to mid-autumn
Soil type:
Lime-free or neutral soil
Sun or Shade:
Does best in full sun
Hardiness:
Minimum temp –23°C (–10°F)

Delphinium grandiflorum

DESCRIPTION

A member of the buttercup (Ranunculaceae) family, Delphinium consists of around 250 species of annuals, biennials and perennials, best known for the intense blue flowers it often produces.

One of the perennial species, *D. grandiflorum* (syn. *D. chinense*) is a native of temperate East Asia. The very finely divided, bright green leaves form a low bushy

foliage clump. The racemes of flowers are usually short and lax, though sometimes they can be quite tall and upright. The vivid blue, long-spurred, 4-petalled flowers are backed by five sepals that can become bract-like. The cultivar 'Tom Pouce' bears bright gentian blue flowers.

Species, variety or cultivar:
'Tom Pouce'
Other common names:
–
Height and spread:
100 x 60 cm (40 x 24 in)
Blooming period:
Summer
Soil type:
Moist, humus-rich, fertile soil
Sun or Shade:
Prefers full sun to part-shade
Hardiness:
Minimum temp –40°C (–40°F)

Dianthus • *Carnation*

DESCRIPTION

Commonly known as carnations or pinks, the 300 or so species in this genus are tufting or spreading perennials largely confined to the Eurasian region. Dianthus is the type genus for its family, the pink (Caryophyllaceae).

Perennial dianthus were among the first plants to be cultivated in European gardens. In medieval times they were grown for their medicinal and flavouring properties as well as for their scent. Since then, countless hybrids have been raised, either as garden plants or for the cut-flower trade. Today we recognize three main groups of dianthus hybrids that are further divided, primarily by flower type. One group, Perpetual-flowering carnations, are the tallest carnations, often with flower stems that need supporting. Not hardy to repeated severe frosts, they are best grown in mild climates for their year-round flowering, and are widely cultivated as greenhouse plants for florists. 'Bright Rendez-vous', a popular fancy cultivar, has creamy white flowers edged with soft pink lacing.

BELOW: Perennial dianthus is similar to annual dianthus in that it prefers cooler temperatures and is planted in dappled shade, just ensure it is protected from the afternoon sun. These flowers can be used anywhere in your garden, especially as a border. The name Dianthus actually means 'divine flowers'.

Species, variety or cultivar:
Perpetual flowering, 'Bright Rendez-vous'

Other common names:
Carnation, Pink

Height and spread:
38 x 30 cm (15 x 12 in)

Blooming period:
Spring

Soil type:
Moist, well-drained, humus-rich soil

Sun or Shade:
Does best in full sun to part-sun

Hardiness:
Minimum temp −12°C (10°F)

Dianthus • *Carnation*

DESCRIPTION

In common with other genera that have a long garden history and have been extensively hybridized, the many Dianthus hybrids and their cultivars are divided into several groups based on growth habit, flower colour and style.

One group, the Pinks, was developed from *D. plumarius*, a species native to eastern and central Europe. The flowers may or may not be fragrant but nearly always have pinked edges. The narrow, somewhat grassy leaves are blue-green – providing a perfect foil for the attractively coloured flowers. The bicoloured cultivar 'Monica Wyatt,' features double flowers that are light pink with a red centre.

Species, variety or cultivar:
  Pink, 'Monica Wyatt'
Other common names:
  Carnation, Pink
Height and spread:
  38 x 30 cm (15 x 12 in)
Blooming period:
  Spring
Soil type:
  Moist, well-drained, humus-rich soil
Sun or Shade:
  Enjoys full sun to part-shade
Hardiness:
  Minimum temp −12°C (10°F)

Dianthus • *Carnation*

Species, variety or cultivar:
  Pink, 'Neon Star'

Other common names:
  Carnation, Pink

Height and spread:
  38 x 30 cm (15 x 12 in)

Blooming period:
  Spring

Soil type:
  Moist, well-drained, humus-rich
  soil

Sun or Shade:
  Enjoys full sun to part-shade

Hardiness:
  Minimum temp –12°C (10°F)

DESCRIPTION

A member of the Pink group of cultivars, 'Neon Star' features an attractive, grassy clump of blue-green foliage, framing the single bright purple-pink flowers. These vibrant flowers emit a lovely fragrance. The name 'pinks' does not refer to the colour but to the ragged petal edges, which appear as if cut with pinking shears. *D. plumarius* is the parent species of Pinks, and they have long been in cultivation. As a general rule, these attractive garden plants require little more maintenance than the removal of spent flowers. Most commonly crossed with *D. plumarius* are the perpetual-flowering carnations, which have given rise to the Allwoodii Pinks.

Dicentra spectabilis • *Bleeding Heart*

DESCRIPTION

The perennial species *D. spectabilis* is a vigorous grower from Japan, northeastern China and Russia's far east. It bears coarsely divided fern-like leaves that disappear in water but redevelop quickly with the arrival of spring. The strongly upright, often red-tinted flower stems carry up to 15 flowers. Borne in clusters above the foliage, the flowers have four petals, the outer pair creating a pouched structure that largely envelops the inner pair. In the case of *D. spectabilis*, each bloom is large, pink and heart-shaped, with slightly protruding white inner petals. The cultivar 'Alba' produces pure white flowers.

LEFT AND BELOW: Dicentra spectabilis 'Alba' has two distinguishing features that set it apart from the regular pink form of the species. The most obvious feature is its white heart-locket flowers, as opposed to the pink of the species. But additionally the leaves are lime-green rather than green, especially in early spring as first emerging are closer in colour to the 'Goldheart' cultivar with startling yellow-green foliage. Since there is no colour to justify calling it 'Bleeding', it is occasionally called 'White Pantaloons', evoking laundry hung out to dry on a line, instead of heart-shaped lockets.

Species, variety or cultivar:
'Alba'
Other common names:
Bleeding Heart
Height and spread:
140 x 100 cm (56 x 40 in)
Blooming period:
Spring
Soil type:
Humus-rich, fertile, well-drained soil
Sun or Shade:
Does best in part-shade
Hardiness:
Minimum temp –23°C (–10°F)

Dictamnus albus • *Burning Bush*

DESCRIPTION

An herbaceous perennial with a woody base, *D. albus* is found from southwestern Europe through to Asia. This clumping plant features bright green compound leaves, composed of up to six pairs of leaflets. The showy white flowers are produced in spikes above the foliage in summer. The whole plant can make you ill if it is ingested, and it exudes a volatile gas that in hot weather can be ignited without harm to the plant, hence one of its common names. Due to its wide distribution, several variants have been named, though the only one currently recognized is *D. a. var. purpureus*.

The cultivar 'Roseus' produces pale pink flowers.

Species, variety or cultivar:
'Roseus'
Other common names:
Burning Bush, Dittany
Height and spread:
90 x 60 cm (36 x 24 in)
Blooming period:
Summer
Soil type:
Moist, humus-rich soil
Sun or Shade:
Enjoys full sun
Hardiness:
Minimum temp –40°C
(–40°F)

Digitalis grandiflora • *Large Yellow Foxglove*

DESCRIPTION

A biennial or short-lived perennial, *D. grandiflora* (syn. *D. ambigua*), is a native of Europe. This easy-to-grow plant forms a basal clump of rather coarse, often elliptical, heavily veined leaves, from the centre of which emerge upright flower stems carrying smaller leaves. The bright green leaves have toothed edges and downy undersides.

Flowering from late spring into summer, the downward-facing, 4-lobed, bell-shaped flowers are pale yellow with darker veining, and open progressively upwards along the spike. Propagate from seed or basal offshoots.

Digitalis species were once widely used in the production of heart stimulant drugs that are now mostly synthesized.

Species, variety or cultivar:
–
Other common names:
Large Yellow Foxglove
Height and spread:
100 x 60 cm (40 x 24 in)
Blooming period:
Late spring to summer
Soil type:
Moist, humus-rich soil
Sun or Shade:
Enjoys full sun to light shade
Hardiness:
Minimum temp –7°C (20°F)

Dodecatheon meadia • *American Cowslip*

DESCRIPTION

Native to North America, Dodecatheon is a charming genus of some 14 species of small herbaceous perennials in the primrose (Primulaceae) family.

From eastern USA, *D. meadia* (syn. *D. pauciflorum*) is a dainty perennial that forms rosettes of oblong leaves. The flowers are produced in heads of 10 to 20, and feature fully reflexed petals, usually coloured purple with a white base, though sometimes they can be pink or white. This plant grows naturally in moist meadows and mountain pastures, and so needs similar conditions in the garden. Propagate from freshly sown seed, although division in late winter, just before it breaks dormancy, is possible.

Species, variety or cultivar:
–

Other common names:
American Cowslip, Eastern Shooting Star, Shooting Star

Height and spread:
45 x 30 cm (18 x 12 in)

Blooming period:
Spring

Soil type:
Cool, moist soil

Sun or Shade:
Prefers full sun to part-shade

Hardiness:
Minimum temp –40°C (–40°F)

Doronicum orientale • *Leopard's Bane*

DESCRIPTION

Commonly know as leopard's bane, the genus Doronicum contains about 35 species of perennial herbs. Native to Europe, southwestern Asia and Siberia, they are members of the daisy (Asteraceae) family.

D. *orientale* (syn. *D. caucasicum*) is a flesh-stemmed perennial from the Caucasus, Lebanon, and southern Europe.It forms clumps of oval basal leaves. Tall slender stems carry the finely rayed, bright yellow daisies – which make a much welcome splash of colour in the garden in spring. These plants are not suitable for hot climates, and are far better adapted to wild and woodland plantings. Propagate by division in autumn.

Species, variety or cultivar:
–
Other common names:
Leopard's Bane
Height and spread:
60 x 30 cm (24 x 12 in)
Blooming period:
Spring
Soil type:
Moderately fertile, well-drained soil
Sun or Shade:
Prefers part-shade
Hardiness:
Minimum temp –29°C (–20°F)

Echinacea purpurea • *Purple Coneflower*

DESCRIPTION

E. purpurea (syn. *Rudbeckia purpurea*) forms a clump of quick-growing, strongly upright stems. The leaves are broad, toothed, deep green, pointed oval to lance-shaped, and can reach up to 15 cm (6 in) long. Dark buds open to reveal reflexed magenta-purple ray florets, to 8 cm (3 in) long, around orange disc florets. This species is the most widely used in herbal medicines. This species grows freely in temperate gardens. Propagate from seed or basal cuttings, or by division. It may self-sow.

'White Swan' is a compact cultivar, reaching up to 50 cm (20 in) tall. It features white flowerheads.

Species, variety or cultivar:
'White Swan'

Other common names:
Purple Coneflower

Height and spread:
50 x 30 cm (20 x 12 in)

Blooming period:
Summer

Soil type:
Well-drained, humus-rich soil

Sun or Shade:
Likes full to part-shade

Hardiness:
Minimum temp –40°C (–40°F)

Epilobium angustifolium • *Fireweed*

DESCRIPTION

There are about 200 species of perennials, annuals, and subshrubs in the genus Epilobium, which belongs to the evening primrose (Onagraceae) family. They are found throughout the world in climates ranging from temperate to tropical or polar, varying greatly in habit.

Found throughout the Northern Hemisphere, *E. angustifolium* (syn. *Chamaenerion angustifolium*) is an invasive vigorous perennial, best suited to wild gardens or areas where it can spread freely. Willowy stems carry narrow, alternately arranged leaves. Racemes of pink or purplish pink 4-petalled flowers are borne in the leaf axils or at the branch tips in summer to early autumn. Propagate from seed or cuttings.

Species, variety or cultivar:
–

Other common names:
Fireweed, French Willow, Great Willow Herb, Rosebay Willow Herb

Height and spread:
2.4 x 2.4 m (8 x 8 ft)

Blooming period:
Summer to early autumn

Soil type:
Moisture-retentive soil

Sun or Shade:
Likes full sun to part-shade

Hardiness:
Minimum temp –40°C (–40°F)

Epimedium x versicolour • *Barrenwort*

DESCRIPTION

Many Epimedium species are relatively new discoveries, most found since 1975. *E. x versicolour* encompasses a range of evergreen clump-forming garden hybrids between *E. grandiflorum* and *E. pinnatum* subsp. *colchicum*. They feature spiny-edged leaves, which are often richly coloured with bronze when young. The flowers have curved spurs that don't exceed the length of the calyx. Though a cool shady spot beneath deciduous trees is one of the best places to position these plants, they can be surprisingly drought tolerant once established. Propagate by division in late winter. The cultivar 'Sulphureum' has bright yellow flowers with slightly longer spurs.

Species, variety or cultivar:
 'Sulphureum'
Other common names:
 Barrenwort, Bishop's Hat,
 Bishop's Mitre, Horny Goat Weed
Height and spread:
 30 x 30 cm (12 x 12 in)
Blooming period:
 Spring
Soil type:
 Humus-rich soil
Sun or Shade:
 Prefers shade
Hardiness:
 Minimum temp –29°C (–20°F)

Eremurus • *Desert Candle*

DESCRIPTION

Belonging to the asphodel (Asphodelaceae) family, the genus Eremurus contains 40 to 50 species of fleshy-stemmed perennials. They are native to western and central Asia, where they grow in dry areas among rocks and in grassland.

Eremurus species hybridize readily, which has resulted in a number of free-flowering hybrid groups in white and shades of pink, amber, orange and yellow. The flowers are borne in tapering spikes and resemble small starry lilies. Their prominently protruding stamens give the spike a soft fluffy appearance. They form basal clumps of strap-shaped leaves. The cultivar 'Cleopatra', produces deep orange flowers.

Species, variety or cultivar:
hybrid cultivar, 'Cleopatra'
Other common names:
Desert Candle
Height and spread:
2 x 1 m (84 x 40 in)
Blooming period:
Summer
Soil type:
Rich, well-drained, sandy soil
Sun or Shade:
Enjoys full sun
Hardiness:
Minimum temp −29°C (−20°F)

Erigeron glaucus • *Beach Aster*

DESCRIPTION

Erigeron is a genus of about 200 species of annuals and perennials belonging to the daisy (Asteraceae) family. The genus is commonly known as fleabane, as some of the species were reputed to repel fleas. They are found throughout temperate regions, particularly in North America, and grow in a variety of habitats. Plant habits vary from very low alpine species, suitable for the rock garden, to robust larger-flowered species growing to 75 cm (30 in) high or more. As a rule, they are undemanding plants, adaptable to a range of soils. Propagate from seed or by division.

From western USA, *E. glaucus* is a somewhat succulent straggly perennial. The broadly oval leaves often have a blue-green cast, and can measure up to 15 cm (6 in) long. The large gold-centred daisy flowers have numerous narrow rays in lilac to violet. It flowers profusely over a long season, chiefly in late spring to early summer.

LEFT: The Beach Aster is at home among rocks on the beach and on ocean cliffs. The flowers are borne from June to September above the unusual, slightly sticky, succulent, pale foliage.

Species, variety or cultivar:
–

Other common names:
Beach Aster, Seaside Daisy

Height and spread:
30 x 60 cm (12 x 24 in)

Blooming period:
Late spring to early summer

Soil type:
Any reasonable well-drained soil

Sun or Shade:
Prefers full sun

Hardiness:
Minimum temp –40°C (–40°F)

Erinus alpinus • *Alpine Balsam*

DESCRIPTION

This species is a cushion-forming herb, native to the Pyrenees and Alps. It has small, spirally arranged leaves, measuring up to 25 mm (1 in) long. They are soft, oblanceolate to wedge-shaped, with toothed or wavy edges, and have a covering of sticky hairs. The inflorescences are racemes, borne at the stem tips. The abundant flowers are shortly tubular, expanding at the mouth into five spreading, purple or white petals. The fruit is a capsule with many seeds. Grown as an alpine this perennial is short-lived, but will self-seed in the rock garden. Propagate from seed or from softwood cuttings taken in spring.

Species, variety or cultivar:
–
Other common names:
Alpine Balsam, Fairy Foxglove
Height and spread:
10 x 15 cm (4 x 6 in)
Blooming period:
Late spring to summer
Soil type:
Well-drained soil
Sun or Shade:
Likes full sun to part-shade
Hardiness:
Minimum temp–34°C (–30°F)

Eriogonum grande • *Wild Buckwheat*

DESCRIPTION

E. grande (syn. *E. latifolium* subsp. *grande*) is a rare, low-growing, shrubby perennial from California. USA. The curling oblong to oval leaves can reach up to 4 in. (10 cm) long, and feature dense white down underneath. Flat-topped heads of small white to pale pink flowers are produced in summer to early autumn. Small, single-seeded, 3-angled fruit follows the flowers. This species makes a good rockery or background plant for drier gardens. Propagate from seed sown in spring or cuttings, or by division of root clumps.

'Rubescens,' is a lower, more sprawling, form, with large leaves and clusters of rose pink flowers.

Species, variety or cultivar:
  'Rubescens'
Other common names:
  Wild Buckwheat
Height and spread:
  60 x 90 cm (24 x 36 in)
Blooming period:
  Summer to early autumn
Soil type:
  Well-drained, preferably sandy soil
Sun or Shade:
  Likes full sun to part-shade
Hardiness:
  Minimum temp −12°C (10°F)

Eryngium variifolium

DESCRIPTION

This evergreen perennial comes from North Africa. The foliage is almost entirely basal, often forming a large clump of white-marbled, dark green, toothed leaves. The thistle-like flowers are held on tall stems during summer. The 25 mm (1 in) wide purple-blue flowerheads are clustered around a central cone, with up to seven narrow, spiny, white-centred bracts. The flowerheads and foliage last well when cut and have a certain charm when dried. This species is most at home in moist, well-drained soil with regular watering during the growing season. Propagate by division or from seed, which germinates readily.

Species, variety or cultivar:
−
Other common names:
−
Height and spread:
75 x 50 cm (30 x 20 in)
Blooming period:
Summer
Soil type:
Moist, well-drained soil
Sun or Shade:
Enjoys full sun to part-shade
Hardiness:
Minimum temp −18°C (0°F)

Euphorbia amygdaloides • *Wood Spurge*

DESCRIPTION

E. amygdaloides is a spreading, mounding, leafy perennial from temperate Eurasia. The soft stems are densely foliaged with spatula-shaped leaves, sometimes more than 8 cm (3 in) long, which are often purple-tinted and carry a slight sheen. Sprays of showy yellow-green bracted flower-heads are produced throughout spring and summer. As with all Euphorbia species, this plant contains a poisonous milky sap which can cause severe skin irritation and, on contact with the eyes, sometimes temporary blindness. The sap has purgative qualities.

The cultivar 'Purpurea' features tall reddish flowerheads and foliage and stems that are strongly tinted with purple-red.

Species, variety or cultivar:
'Purpurea'

Other common names:
Wood Spurge

Height and spread:
80 x 100 cm (32 x 40 in)

Blooming period:
Spring and summer

Soil type:
Well-drained soil

Sun or Shade:
Prefers full sun to part-shade

Hardiness:
Minimum temp –7°C (20°F)

Evolvulus glomeratus

DESCRIPTION

This evergreen perennial is found in Brazil and some neighbouring countries. It features a dense mound of foliage emerging from a mass of rhizomes. The grey-green leaves have a covering of soft silky hairs. From spring to autumn, it produces a long succession of brilliant blue flowers with a small white eye. The 25 mm (1 in) wide flowers tend to wilt after noon in hot weather. The flowers are followed by dry seed capsules that are spherical to ovate and contain up to four small seeds. Propagate by root division or from cuttings. This plant is a popular subject for basket culture.

Species, variety or cultivar:
–

Other common names:
–

Height and spread:
45 x 90 cm (18 x 36 in)

Blooming period:
Spring to autumn

Soil type:
Well-drained soil

Sun or Shade:
Enjoys full sun

Hardiness:
Minimum temp –7°C (20°F)

Felicia amelloides • *Blue Daisy*

Species, variety or cultivar:
–

Other common names:
Blue Daisy, Blue Marguerite

Height and spread:
60 x 60 cm (24 x 24 in)

Blooming period:
Summer

Soil type:
Moderately fertile soil

Sun or Shade:
Enjoys full sun

Hardiness:
Minimum temp –7°C (20°F)

DESCRIPTION

From South Africa, *F. amelloides* (syn. *Agathaea coelestis, F. aethiopica*) is an evergreen subshrub with trailing and/or upright stems. The light green leaves have a covering of very fine hairs. It is grown for the ornamental value of its summer flowers, which are borne singly and feature vivid yellow disc florets and light blue ray florets. This species will grow outdoors, preferring open, sunny, low-humidity areas; it may die off in prolonged damp conditions. In containers they need a loam-based compost with some added grit for drainage. Propagate from seeds sown in spring, or by taking stem-tip cuttings in summer, and overwintering in frost-free conditions.

Filipendula vulgaris • *Dropwort*

DESCRIPTION

The genus Filipendula contains about ten species of fleshy-stemmed or tuberous clump-forming perennials, and is a member of the rose (Rosaceae) family.

F. vulgaris (syn. *F. hexapetala*) is a tuberous clump-forming perennial from Europe and northern and central Asia. It is usually found growing in damp habitats, but has some tolerance to drier conditions. A tall attractive plant, it has very deeply cut fern-like leaves. In summer, it produces feathery plumes of small, white, 5-petalled flowers, which are often tinged reddish purple. Small single-seeded fruit follow the flowers. Propagate from seed or by division.

Species, variety or cultivar:
–
Other common names:
Dropwort
Height and spread:
90 x 45 cm (36 x 18 in)
Blooming period:
Summer
Soil type:
Moist, humus-rich soil
Sun or Shade:
Prefers part-shade
Hardiness:
Minimum temp –40°C (–40°F)

Foeniculum vulgare • *Fennel*

DESCRIPTION

Familiar as a culinary herb and in many areas as a weed of waste ground, Foeniculum is a member of the carrot (Apiaceae) family. The sole species in the genus, *F. vulgare*, is a pungently aromatic biennial or perennial, found naturally in Europe and around the Mediterranean. It forms a clump of erect hollow stems with feathery foliage made up of many hair-like deep green to bronze leaflets. Heads of small yellow flowers appear through summer and then dry to become similarly shaped pale brown seed heads.

The cultivar 'Purpureum' (syn. 'Bronze', 'Purpurascens') features dark purplish maroon to bronze foliage.

Species, variety or cultivar:
  'Purpureum'
Other common names:
  Fennel
Height and spread:
  2 x 0.9 m (7 x 3 ft)
Blooming period:
  Summer
Soil type:
  Moderately fertile soil
Sun or Shade:
  Enjoys full sun
Hardiness:
  Minimum temp –29°C (–20°F)

Gaillardia x grandiflora • *Blanket Flower*

DESCRIPTION

The genus Gaillardia was discovered in the Rocky Mountains around 1825 by David Douglas and named for a French patron, Gaillard de Charentonneau (sometimes given as Marentonneau). The genus contains around 30 species of annual, biennial and perennial daisies (family Asteraceae), and occurs mainly in southern USA and Mexico. The common name blanket flower comes from a Native American legend of a blanket maker whom the spirits rewarded with an ever-blooming blanket of flowers on his grave.

G. x grandiflora is a garden hybrid between *G. aristata* and *G. pulchella*. While very similar to *G. aristata*, it is often slightly larger and generally more vigorous, hardier and heavier flowering. Propagate from seed or basal cuttings, or by division. This plant is so easily cultivated that replacing any winter casualties is no problem.

'Burgunder' (syn. 'Burgundy'), one of the many cultivars of this attractive plant, produces deep red flowers.

BELOW: *Gaillardia x grandiflora* 'Goblin'. These plants grow best in sunny situations having a well-drained soil. They are useful on dry sites but will be short-lived on moist, fertile or heavy soils. Remove the flowers as they fade to keep the plant flowering. Blanket Flower is not long-lived and will have problems with powdery mildew and aster yellows.

Species, variety or cultivar:
  'Burgunder'
Other common names:
  Blanket Flower, Firewheel
Height and spread:
  60 x 100 cm (24 x 40 in)
Blooming period:
  Summer and autumn
Soil type:
  Gritty, well-drained soil
Sun or Shade:
  Prefers full sun
Hardiness:
  Minimum temp –29°C (–20°F)

Galtonia candicans • *Summer Hyacinth*

DESCRIPTION

One of three species of bulbous perennials in this genus belonging to the lily (Liliaceae) family, *G. candicans* comes from Free State and KwaZulu-Natal in South Africa, and Lesotho. The leaves, which are rather fleshy and strap-shaped, and reach up to 75 cm (30 in) long, form a basal clump. They are grown for their tall spires of drooping bell-

shaped flowers, which bloom in late summer. The fragrant flowers are white, tinged green at the base.

This plant dislikes being disturbed and bulbs will rot in winter in wet ground. Protect new growth from snails. Propagate from seed or careful division of offsets.

Species, variety or cultivar:
  –
Other common names:
  Summer hyacinth
Height and spread:
  120 x 30 cm (48 x 12 in)
Blooming period:
  Late summer
Soil type:
  Light, fertile, well-drained soil
Sun or Shade:
  Prefers full sun
Hardiness:
  Minimum temp –29°C (–20°F)

Gaura lindheimeri

DESCRIPTION

A vigorous heavy-flowering perennial, *G. lindheimeri* is native to Texas and Louisiana, USA. It forms a clump of upright stems with narrow, elliptical, toothed leaves less than 12 mm (½ in) long. Emerging from the clump of leaves are the tall wiry flower stems. These stems carry sprays of graceful, airy, 4-petalled, pink-tinted white flowers that are nearly 25 mm (1 in) wide, and feature large and wing-like upper petals. Remove spent flowers regularly, and cut back hard after flowering. Propagate from seed or basal cuttings.

Growing to 60 cm (24 in) tall, 'Whirling Butterflies' is a very heavy-blooming cultivar that features large flowers.

Species, variety or cultivar:
  'Whirling Butterflies'
Other common names:
  –
Height and spread:
  150 × 100 cm (60 × 40 in)
Blooming period:
  Spring to summer
Soil type:
  Light, gritty, well-drained soil
Sun or Shade:
  Prefers full sun to part-shade
Hardiness:
  Minimum temp –29°C (–20°F)

Gazania rigens • *Treasure Flower*

DESCRIPTION

This perennial has fleshy stems that strike root as they spread, forming a large leafy clump. The narrow lance-shaped leaves can measure over 10 cm (4 in). They are smooth-edged or near-pinnately lobed, deep green to bronze above, with a covering of white hair on the undersides. Held on long stems, the flowerheads are up to 8 cm (3 in) wide. The ray florets are orange with a black base, the disc florets are orange-brown. Propagate by division, or from basal cuttings or seed.

The name Gazania comes from Theodore of Gaza (1398–1478), who translated the botanical texts of Theophrastus from Greek into Latin.

Species, variety or cultivar:
–

Other common names:
Treasure Flower

Height and spread:
20 x 100 cm (8 x 40 in)

Blooming period:
Late spring to summer

Soil type:
Gritty, very free-draining soil

Sun or Shade:
Prefers full sun

Hardiness:
Minimum temp –7°C (20°F)

Gentiana ternifolia • *Gentian*

DESCRIPTION

This spreading autumn-flowering perennial is native to western China. The narrow lance-shaped leaves, to nearly 18 mm (¾ in) long, form loose basal rosettes. The flower stems are often erect at the tips and carry 40 mm (1¾ in) long, funnel-shaped flowers in mid-blue, marked green and white. This plant prefers a climate with distinct seasons. Propagate by division or from seed.

Some gentians have medicinal uses and the genus name honors Gentius, King of Illyria, who in 180 BC was cited by Pliny as having discovered these properties. Modern herbalists use root extracts to treat anemia and it is also a flavouring.

Species, variety or cultivar:
–
Other common names:
Gentian
Height and spread:
20 x 40 cm (8 x 16 in)
Blooming period:
Autumn
Soil type:
Moist, well-drained, humus-rich soil
Sun or Shade:
Prefers half-sun
Hardiness:
Minimum temp –12°C (10°F)

Geranium • *Cranesbill*

DESCRIPTION

The plants often called geraniums in fact belong in the genus Pelargonium. While both genera are in the geranium (Geraniaceae) family, true geraniums are a very different group of some 300 species of perennials and subshrubs, sometimes evergreen, that are widespread in temperate zones. The name Geranium comes from the Greek *geranos* (crane), referring to the fruit's resemblance to the shape of a crane's bill. Herb Robert (*G. robertianum*) and others have a long history in herbal medicine for a wide range of ailments and uses. Propagate from seed, cuttings or by division. Most geraniums are hardy and will grow in a wide range of conditions.

Geraniums tend to sport readily and interbreed freely, so there are many garden forms in a wide range of sizes and flower colours. One of the many popular hybrid cultivars is 'Ann Folkard', which has a trailing habit, yellow-green foliage and dark-centred magenta flowers.

Species, variety or cultivar:
hybrid cultivar, 'Ann Folkard'
Other common names:
Cranesbill
Height and spread:
90 x 120 cm (36 x 48 in)
Blooming period:
Summer
Soil type:
Moist, humus-rich soil
Sun or Shade:
Likes full sun to part-shade
Hardiness:
Minimum temp –23°C (10°F)

Geranium pratense • *Cranesbill*

DESCRIPTION

G. pratense is a sturdy spreading perennial
found from central Europe to the western
Himalayas. It features upright stems, with
10–20 cm (4–8 in) wide, dark green leaves that
take on rich golden tones in autumn. Each leaf
has seven to nine deep pinnate lobes with
toothed edges. The flowerheads can be
crowded to rather open, carrying mauve-blue
flowers that are nearly 50 mm (2 in) wide and
are often heavily veined. Propagate from seed,
cuttings or by division. May self-sow.

The cultivar 'Mrs Kendall Clark' has
delicate mauve flowers finely etched with
translucent veins.

Species, variety or cultivar:
   'Mrs Kendall Clark'
Other common names:
   Cranesbill
Height and spread:
   120 x 100 cm (48 x 40 in)
Blooming period:
   Summer
Soil type:
   Moist, humus-rich soil
Sun or Shade:
   Likes full sun to part-shade
Hardiness:
   Minimum temp –29°C (–20°F)

Geranium versicolor • *Cranesbill*

DESCRIPTION

Found from Sicily to the Balkans and Greece, *G. versicolor* is a mounding and spreading perennial. The stems and foliage are coated with bristles. The leaves are largest at the base, measuring up to 20 cm (8 in) wide, becoming smaller higher up the plant. Each of the leaves has five pinnate toothed lobes. Blooming in summer, this plant bears airy sprays of magenta-veined white flowers. The flowers develop into long narrow fruits. Care should be taken when selecting a site for these plants, as the roots can be invasive. Propagate from seed, cuttings or by division. The cultivar 'Snow White' has pure white flowers.

Species, variety or cultivar:
'Snow White'
Other common names:
Cranesbill
Height and spread:
20 x 80 cm (8 x 32 in)
Blooming period:
Summer
Soil type:
Moist, humus-rich soil
Sun or Shade:
Likes full sun to part-shade
Hardiness:
Minimum temp –23°C (–10°F)

Geum • *Avens*

DESCRIPTION

A member of the rose (Rosaceae) family, the genus Geum contains around 40 species and is widely distributed in the temperate regions. They are either rosette-forming or spread by rhizomes or runners, with their fine hairy pinnate or lobed leaves arising directly from the roots. The showy flowers resemble tiny single roses.

Geums hybridize quite freely, and although many of the garden forms can be traced back to G. *chiloense*, some have more complicated parentage and are classified separately. One of the many popular hybrids is 'Beech House Apricot,' with 20 cm (8 in) tall flower stems carrying light apricot-pink flowers.

Species, variety or cultivar:
  hybrid cultivar, 'Beech House Apricot'
Other common names:
  Avens
Height and spread:
  60 x 90 cm (24 x 36 in)
Blooming period:
  Late winter to late summer
Soil type:
  Moist, well-drained soil
Sun or Shade:
  Enjoys full sun to part-shade
Hardiness:
  Minimum temp –23°C (–10°F)

Glaucium flavum • *Yellow-horned Poppy*

DESCRIPTION

This biennial or short-lived perennial comes from Europe, North Africa and the Middle East. Fine hairs cover the pinnately lobed, toothed, blue-green leaves, which form a basal rosette. Branching flower stems with small leaves emerge from the rosette in summer, and carry 4-petalled flowers, usually 5 cm (2 in) wide, in shades of bright yellow or orange. The poppy-like flowers are followed by very narrow curved seed pods, to 30 cm (12 in) long. This plant is very easily grown in any temperate climate with reasonably warm summers. Propagate from seed – this species may self-sow, though rarely invasively.

Species, variety or cultivar:
–

Other common names:
Yellow-horned Poppy

Height and spread:
100 x 40 cm (40 x 16 in)

Blooming period:
Summer

Soil type:
Light, rather gritty, free-draining soil

Sun or Shade:
Enjoys full sun

Hardiness:
Minimum temp –18°C (0°F)

Gypsophila repens • *Baby's Breath*

DESCRIPTION

Related to the pink (Caryophyllaceae) family, the 100-odd annuals and perennials in the genus Gypsophila occur naturally in temperate Eurasia. Commonly known as baby's breath for their sweetly scented flowers, they range from spreading mat-forming plants to upright shrubby species.

One of the mat-forming perennials, *G. repens* comes from the mountains of central and southern Europe. It has narrow, pointed oval, blue-green leaves to over 12 mm (½ in) long and produces sprays of up to 25 tiny, white, pink or mauve flowers. Propagate from basal cuttings or seed. The cultivar 'Rosa Schönheit' (syn. 'Rose Beauty') bears deep pink flowers.

Species, variety or cultivar:
'Rosa Schönheit'

Other common names:
Baby's Breath

Height and spread:
10 x 60 cm (4 x 24 in)

Blooming period:
Summer

Soil type:
Fertile, moist, well-drained soil, neutral to slightly alkaline

Sun or Shade:
Likes full sun to part-shade

Hardiness:
Minimum temp –34°C (–30°F)

Helenium autumnale • *Sneezeweed*

DESCRIPTION

This North American perennial makes a dense clump of stems with narrow, usually serrated, leaves to 15 cm (6 in) long. Held above the foliage are the abundant, 5 cm (2 in) wide, bright yellow to golden flowerheads, each with up to 20 reflexed ray florets around a central cone of disc florets. Routine deadheading prolongs flowering; alternatively use as a cut flower to encourage repeat flowering. Propagate by division, or from basal cuttings or seed.

It is known as sneezeweed not because it causes allergies, but from the use by Native Americans of the powdered flowers to make snuff.

Species, variety or cultivar:
–

Other common names:
Sneezeweed

Height and spread:
1.5 x 0.9 m (5 x 3 ft)

Blooming period:
Mid-summer to mid-autumn

Soil type:
Moist, well-drained soil

Sun or Shade:
Likes full sun

Hardiness:
Minimum temp –40°C (–40°F)

Helianthus salicifolius

DESCRIPTION

Commonly known as sunflowers, Helianthus members are so-called not so much for the shape of the blooms as for the way the flowerheads turn to follow the sun. This genus of 70 annuals and perennials in the daisy (Asteraceae) family is from the Americas.

H. salicifolius is a perennial native to south-central USA. The drooping, narrowly lance-shaped leaves can reach up to 20 cm (8 in) long and are slightly hairy. Held high above the foliage are the distinctive flowerheads with yellow ray florets around a dark disc. Propagate from seed, basal cuttings or by division.

Species, variety or cultivar:
–
Other common names:
–
Height and spread:
3 x 1.2 m (10 x 4 ft)
Blooming period:
Autumn
Soil type:
Fertile, moist, well-drained soil
Sun or Shade:
Enjoys full sun
Hardiness:
Minimum temp –34°C (–30°F)

Heliopsis helianthoides • *Everlasting Sunflower*

DESCRIPTION

The name Heliopsis means 'resembling a sunflower.' Native to North America, this genus of 13 species of loosely branched, erect, perennial herbs belongs to the daisy (Asteraceae) family.

H. helianthoides is a perennial found from Ontario, Canada, to Florida and Mississippi, USA. The 15 cm (6 in) long mid-green leaves are smooth, oval- to sword-shaped, and coarsely toothed. Numerous terminal flowerheads of bright yellow daisy-like flowers are produced from mid-summer to autumn. Propagate from seed or divide clumps periodically in spring or autumn.

H. h. var. scabra has very rough stems and leaves. It produces double orange-yellow flowers over a long blooming period.

Species, variety or cultivar:
var. scabra

Other common names:
Everlasting Sunflower, False Sunflower, Smooth Ox-eye

Height and spread:
150 x 60 cm (60 x 24 in)

Blooming period:
Mid-summer to autumn

Soil type:
Fertile, moist, well-drained soil

Sun or Shade:
Prefers full sun

Hardiness:
Minimum temp –40°C (–40°F)

Helleborus niger • *Christmas Rose*

DESCRIPTION

This winter- to spring-flowering evergreen perennial is found from northern Italy to southern Germany. The deep green leaves are leathery and serrated, with five to nine broad leaflets, to 20 cm (8 in) long. Held on long stems, the white flowers are flushed with purple-red. The simple, 5-petalled, bowl-shaped flowers open flat, revealing prominent greenish nectaries and many yellow stamens at their centre.

This plant will benefit from having old foliage removed when dormant, and the removal of spent flowerheads once the seeds have fallen. Take care when tending to pruning and trimming tasks as this plant is toxic, and the sap can irritate the skin. Propagation is by division or from seed, which may require two periods of stratification. Christmas Rose naturalizes in suitable climates. It prefers woodland conditions where it will enjoy a position in dappled shade. It can prove a difficult garden subject, and may need added protection in winter.

BELOW: The Christmas Rose (*Helleborus niger*) is one of the easiest and most rewarding garden plants to grow. Their ability to bloom in the darkest months of the year when everything else is frozen solid make them a valuable asset to any garden.

Species, variety or cultivar:
–

Other common names:
Christmas Rose

Height and spread:
30 x 50 cm (12 x 20 in)

Blooming period:
Mid-winter to spring

Soil type:
Deep, fertile, humus-rich, well-drained soil

Sun or Shade:
Prefers full shade to part-shade

Hardiness:
Minimum temp –40°C (–40°F)

Hemerocallis citrina • *Daylily*

DESCRIPTION

Hemerocallis species are known as daylilies, and are so-named because each of their funnel- to bell-shaped flowers last just one day, though they carry a succession of blooms from late spring until autumn.

 H. citrina is a Chinese species with narrow leaves to 1.2 m (4 ft) long and flower stems that are upright, branching from above half height, and bearing up to 50 plus fragrant pale yellow flowers to over 10 cm (4 in) wide. The flowers open at night and stay open for most of the next day. They are easily grown in a sunny or part-shaded position with moist, fertile, well-drained soil.

Species, variety or cultivar:
 –
Other common names:
 Daylily
Height and spread:
 1.5 x 2 m (5 x 7 ft)
Blooming period:
 Late spring to autumn
Soil type:
 Fertile, moist, well-drained soil
Sun or Shade:
 Enjoys full sun to part-shade
Hardiness:
 Minimum temp –34°C (–30°F)

Hemerocallis • *Daylily*

DESCRIPTION

Daylilies hybridize readily and with such beautiful flowers it should not come as a surprise to find that there are several hundred hybrids and cultivars covering a wide range of flower colours and plant sizes, from miniatures around 30 cm (12 in) tall to those with 1.2 m (4 ft) flower stems. All parts, especially the buds and flowers, are edible and may be added to salads or used as a colourful garnish. The stamens can be used as a saffron colour substitute.

The cultivar 'Cartwheels' grows to 75 cm (30 in) tall, and features large bright yellow flowers accented with a light mid-stripe.

Species, variety or cultivar:
  hybrid cultivar, 'Cartwheels'
Other common names:
  Daylily
Height and spread:
  75 cm x unlimited (30 in x unlimited)
Blooming period:
  Late spring to autumn
Soil type:
  Fertile, moist, well-drained soil
Sun or Shade:
  Enjoys full sun to part-shade
Hardiness: Minimum temp –34°C (–30°F)

Heterotheca mucronatum • *Golden Aster*

DESCRIPTION

The genus Heterotheca is commonly known as the golden aster, and is a member of the daisy (Asteraceae) family. One of 30 species in the genus, *H. mucronatum* is a low-growing perennial herb from North America. It bears greyish green lance-shaped leaves. Throughout summer and autumn, it produces erect clusters of flowerheads with golden yellow daisy-like flowers. The fruit that follows the flowers is a scaly and bristly achene (one-seeded fruit).

The low-growing habit of this plant makes it well suited for garden edging. In favourable conditions it requires minimal maintenance, needing only light watering. Propagate from seed, or by division in spring.

Species, variety or cultivar:
–
Other common names:
Golden Aster
Height and spread:
30 x 20 cm (12 x 8 in)
Blooming period:
Summer and autumn
Soil type:
Well-drained, moist soil
Sun or Shade:
Prefers full sun
Hardiness:
Minimum temp –40°C (–40°F)

Heuchera x brizoides • *Coral Bells*

DESCRIPTION

H. x brizoides encompasses a group of hybrids that share *H. sanguinea* as one parent, the others being *H. micrantha*, *H. americana*, and perhaps others. They are a mixed group, differing mainly in flower colour. They form a dense clump of basal foliage of simple, green, lobed, heart-shaped leaves on thin wiry stalks. The branching flower stems carry sprays of tiny, usually 5-petalled, flowers from late spring to autumn. Propagate by division or from seed, sown fresh in early autumn.

Featuring graceful, airy flowerheads available in many shades of pink, red and white, the Bressingham hybrids are particularly popular.

Species, variety or cultivar:
  Bressingham hybrid
Other common names:
  Alum Root, Coral Bells
Height and spread:
  75 x 45 cm (30 x 18 in)
Blooming period:
  Late spring to autumn
Soil type:
  Fertile, moist, humus-rich, well-drained soil
Sun or Shade:
  Likes full sun to part-shade
Hardiness:
  Minimum temp –34°C (–30°F)

Hibiscus trionum • *Flower-of-an-Hour*

DESCRIPTION

This short-lived perennial or annual is found in Australia, New Zealand and tropical regions of Africa and Asia. It is one of over 200 annual or perennial herbs, shrubs or trees in the genus Hibiscus, which is widely distributed throughout warm-temperate, subtropical and tropical regions of the world. The simple alternate lobed leaves are carried on slightly hairy stems. The open bell-shaped flowers are creamy yellow with a crimson-black eye and a prominent staminal column. The fruit is a capsule.

To maintain an attractive shape, prune this plant back hard after flowering. Propagate from seed or by division.

Species, variety or cultivar:
–

Other common names:
Flower-of-an-Hour

Height and spread:
60 x 30 cm (24 x 12 in)

Blooming period:
Summer to autumn

Soil type:
Rich, moist soil

Sun or Shade:
Enjoys full sun

Hardiness:
Minimum temp –1°C (30°F)

Hosta plantaginea • *August Lily*

DESCRIPTION

Unlike most hostas, *H. plantaginea* is grown as much for its flowers as for its foliage. A clump-forming plant from China and Japan, it features elegant bright green leaves, with the wavy surface deeply etched by veins. Measuring up to 25 cm (10 in) long, these lance-shaped leaves taper to a fine point. Stiff stems carry small racemes of large, funnel-shaped, white flowers that are sometimes mauve-tinted, and emit a pleasant fragrance.

This plant makes an ideal subject for container planting. For best results, water and feed well during the growing season. Propagate by dividing as the first buds show.

Species, variety or cultivar:
–
Other common names:
August Lily, Maruba
Height and spread:
65 x 80 cm (26 x 32 in)
Blooming period:
Mid-summer
Soil type:
Moist, cool, humus-rich, well-drained soil
Sun or Shade:
Prefers shade to part-shade
Hardiness:
Minimum temp –12°C (10°F)

Hosta sieboldii • *Koba Giboshi*

DESCRIPTION

This clump-forming perennial from Japan and Sakhalin Island is grown primarily for its impressive foliage. Tapering to a fine point, the lance-shaped leaves can be up to 15 cm (6 in) long, often with an undulating and puckered surface. These deep green leaves feature an attractive border of crisp white. In mid-summer, the dainty, funnel-shaped, mauve flowers make an appearance, held above the foliage on tall stiff stems.

These plants appreciate a little extra attention during the growing season. Ensure they are adequately watered and supplied with nutrients during this time. When the first buds appear, the clump can be divided.

Species, variety or cultivar:
–

Other common names:
Koba Giboshi

Height and spread:
50 x 80 cm (20 x 32 in)

Blooming period:
Mid-summer

Soil type:
Moist, cool, humus-rich, well-drained soil

Sun or Shade:
Prefers shade to part-shade

Hardiness:
Minimum temp –29°C (–20°F)

Houttuynia cordata • *Rainbow Plant*

DESCRIPTION

The sole member of the genus, *H. cordata* is a widely spreading herbaceous perennial from the swamps and damp margins of China and Japan. Below ground it produces thong-like questing rhizomes. The aromatic heart-shaped leaves, reaching up to 9 cm (3½ in) long, are deep green, often stained burgundy. Clusters of tiny yellow flowers, surrounded by four white petal-like bracts, are carried atop red stems from mid-summer onwards. Propagate by division. It can become quite invasive and hard to remove.

'Chameleon' (syns 'Court Jester,' 'Tricolor', 'Variegata') is a slightly less vigorous clone with leaves broadly edged in yellow and stained red.

Species, variety or cultivar:
  'Chameleon'
Other common names:
  Rainbow Plant, Chameleon Plant
Height and spread:
  30 x 100 cm (12 x 40 in)
Blooming period:
  Mid-summer
Soil type:
  Moist to wet soil
Sun or Shade:
  Likes full sun to part-shade
Hardiness:
  Minimum temp –29°C (–20°F)

Hyssopsus officinalis • *Hyssop*

DESCRIPTION

While there are ten species of perennials or small shrubs in the genus Hyssopsus, a member of the mint (Lamiaceae) family, the most commonly grown species is *H. officinalis*. This variable shrubby perennial originated in southern and eastern Europe and is naturalized in USA. The opposite leaves are lance-shaped and very aromatic. In late summer, rather sparse thin flower spikes bear the violet to blue, 2-lipped, tubular flowers typical of the mint family. This plant is an ideal choice for low hedging. Pinch growing tips to encourage bushiness. Propagate from seed or cuttings. The cultivar 'Sissinghurst' has a dwarf, compact habit.

Species, variety or cultivar:
  'Sissinghurst'
Other common names:
  Hyssop
Height and spread:
  60 x 30 cm (24 x 12 in)
Blooming period:
  Late summer
Soil type:
  Well-drained soil
Sun or Shade:
  Prefers full sun
Hardiness:
  Minimum temp –40°C (–40°F)

Iberis sempervirens • *Candytuft*

DESCRIPTION

There are 30-odd annuals, perennials and subshrubs in the genus Iberis, which belongs to the cabbage (Brassicaceae) family. *I. sempervirens* is a spreading evergreen species from southern Europe, with small, oblong, dark green leaves that are mainly clustered at the stem tips. Blooming throughout spring and summer, the 5 cm (2 in) wide flowerheads, which are most often white, are carried on short stems that hold them clear of the foliage. When not in flower, this plant forms an attractive rounded bush.

Regular removal of spent flowers will encourage continuous blooming. Propagate from seed or small cuttings.

Species, variety or cultivar:
–

Other common names:
Candytuft

Height and spread:
30 x 60 cm (12 x 24 in)

Blooming period:
Spring and summer

Soil type:
Light, moist, well-drained soil

Sun or Shade:
Enjoys full sun to part-shade

Hardiness:
Minimum temp –18°C (0°F)

Incarvillea emodi

DESCRIPTION

The genus Incarvillea contains 14 species from central and eastern Asia, and belongs to the trumpet-vine (Bignoniaceae) family. Hailing from Afghanistan, Pakistan and into northern India, *I. emodi* is a rosette-forming perennial with large mid-green leaves. In spring it produces stems of deep pink trumpets, flared at the edges, with a yellow throat, each bloom 6 cm (2½ in) long.

This plant needs to be positioned in a spot offering shelter from the hottest afternoon sun. In return it will reward by adding an exotic element to the garden over its long blooming period. Propagation is from fresh seed; careful division is also possible although established plants resent disturbance.

Species, variety or cultivar:
–
Other common names:
–
Height and spread:
50 x 40 cm (20 x 16 in)
Blooming period:
Spring
Soil type:
Moisture-retentive soil
Sun or Shade:
Prefers part-shade
Hardiness:
Minimum temp –18°C (0°F)

Inula grandiflora

DESCRIPTION

Members of this large genus in the daisy (Asteraceae) family are found in a wide range of habitats, from dry mountainsides to moist shaded sites, from Europe through to subtropical Africa and Asia. Most are herbaceous perennials, with some biennials and annuals.

I. grandiflora (syns *I. glandulosa, I. orientalis*) is an almost shrubby species from the Caucasus region. The smooth-edged leaves, to 12 cm (5 in) long, bear yellow to brown hairs, and are densely covered in minute glands. The trademark yellow daisy flowers, to 8 cm (3 in) across, are produced throughout summer. Propagate from seed or by division.

Species, variety or cultivar:
–
Other common names:
–
Height and spread:
60 x 100 cm (24 x 40 in)
Blooming period:
Summer
Soil type:
Rich, moist soil
Sun or Shade:
Likes full sun
Hardiness:
Minimum temp –23°C (–10°F)

Iris ensata • *Japanese Water Iris*

DESCRIPTION

Iris is the type genus for the family Iridaceae, taking its name from the Greek goddess of the rainbow. Commonly known as the Japanese iris or woodland iris, *I. ensata* (syn. *I. kaempferi*) comes from Europe, Asia and North America. Woodland irises thrive in dappled sunlight with moist well-drained soil, and are not tolerant of dry hot conditions. The tall, dark green, strappy leaves are grass-like and feature a distinctive mid-vein. Held well above the foliage, are the single, occasionally branched, stems of 6-petalled beardless flowers, which vary in colour from red, purple or blue. These attractive blooms appear in early summer. Woodland irises will grow in shallow water. Propagation is usually by division when dormant, less commonly by seed.

A range of cultivars has been developed from *I. ensata*. 'Dresden Blue' features rich blue standards and falls. The falls are highlighted with golden yellow tones near the base.

BELOW: *Iris ensata* 'Blueberry Rim'. The Japanese iris is the largest flowers of all irises, some being about 30 cm (12 in) across. They have been grown for over 200 years in Japan and also during the last century in the USA. So today, there is a range of flower shapes and patterns, as well as a range of colours.

Species, variety or cultivar:
   'Dresden Blue'
Other common names:
   Japanese Water Iris, Woodland Iris
Height and spread:
   90 x 100 cm (36 x 40 in)
Blooming period:
   Early summer
Soil type:
   Moist, well-drained soil
Sun or Shade:
   Enjoys full sun
Hardiness:
   Minimum temp –29°C (–20°F)

Iris unguicularis • *Algerian Iris*

DESCRIPTION

I. unguicularis (syn. *I. stylosa*) is an evergreen species from Greece, Turkey, western Syria, Algeria and some of the Mediterranean islands. Indicative of its origins, it grows well in hot dry aspects. The flowers are borne from winter to early spring, though they

are usually well hidden among the clump of tough, narrow, grassy leaves. The blooms are usually pale lavender-blue, with the falls featuring gold markings at the base. To best enjoy the attractive fragrant flowers, trim back the foliage in early winter. Many cultivars have been developed from this species. Propagate by division when dormant.

Species, variety or cultivar:
–
Other common names:
Algerian Iris, Winter Iris
Height and spread:
38 x 50 cm (15 x 20 in)
Blooming period:
Winter to early spring
Soil type:
Moist, well-drained soil
Sun or Shade:
Likes full sun to part-shade
Hardiness:
Minimum temp –18°C (0°F)

Iris • *Bearded Iris*

DESCRIPTION

Irises have been cultivated since the time of the Egyptian pharaoh Thutmosis I, around 1500 BC.

The bearded hybrids are hardy perennials grown from rhizomes. They will survive in most climates but produce more flowers in cold climates. The upright pale blue-green foliage sits above the ground, while the large spikes of flowers appear in late spring and come in a range of colours. The flowers have standards and falls, with a distinctive beard on each bloom. Divide every five to seven years.

One of the Tall Bearded Irises, 'Exotic Isle' has dark purple flowers, the falls marked with white and gold.

Species, variety, or cultivar
  Tall Bearded Hybrid, 'Exotic Isle'
Other common names:
  Bearded Iris
Height and spread:
  100 x 90 cm (40 x 36 in)
Blooming period:
  Late spring
Soil type:
  Fertile, well-drained soil
Sun or Shade:
  Enjoys full sun
Hardiness:
  Minimum temp –7°C (20°F)

Jaborosa integrifolia

DESCRIPTION

The about 20 scrambling, evergreen, perennial herbs from South America in this genus are members of the nightshade (Solanaceae) family. The leaves arise from a central base, and clusters of 5-lobed, bell-shaped or tubular flowers, are solitary or in few-flowered cymes.

J. integrifolia is a tuft-forming perennial growing from an underground trailing stem, native to southern Brazil, Uruguay and Argentina. Simple, narrowly oval-shaped leaves, to 15 cm (6 in) long, grow on long stalks. Large, solitary, tubular green to white, narrow-lobed flowers, to 6 cm (2½ in) in diameter, are borne in summer and are fragrant at night.

Species, variety or cultivar:
–
Other common names:
–
Height and spread:
20 x 20 cm (8 x 8 in)
Blooming period:
Summer
Soil type:
Moist soil kept drier in winter
Sun or Shade:
Likes a partly shaded position
Hardiness:
Minimum temp –18°C (0°F)

Kirengeshoma palmata

DESCRIPTION

A genus of a single species in the hydrangea (Hydrangeaceae) family, this charming woodland perennial is from Japan and Korea. An elegant, arching, herbaceous perennial, it has large, maple-like, soft green leaves 20 cm (8 in) long along black stems. In summer, pale lemon, drooping, thick-petalled flowers, shaped somewhat like shuttlecocks hover above the foliage in groups of three, with five petals per bloom. This species needs to be given a cool shaded aspect in moist, humus-rich soil sheltered from winds. Propagate from seed freshly sown or by careful division of established clumps.

Species, variety or cultivar:
–
Other common names:
–
Height and spread:
120 x 75 cm (48 x 30 in)
Blooming period:
Summer
Soil type:
Moist, humus-rich soil
Sun or Shade:
Prefers a cool shaded aspect
Hardiness:
Minimum temp –7°C (20°F)

Kniphofia caulescens • *Red-Hot Poker*

DESCRIPTION

Most of the nearly 70 species in this genus in the asphodel (Asphodelaceae) family are South African, clump-forming perennials with grassy to sword-shaped, often evergreen foliage that emerges from vigorous rhizomes. They are grown for their mainly autumn to spring spikes of intensely coloured, usually orange and/or yellow, flowers, borne in bottlebrush heads at the top of strong, tall, upright stems.

K. caulescens is a tough alpine species with evergreen, narrow but thick blue-green leaves. Coppery flower stems support 30 cm (12 in) long, densely packed heads of pink-tinted cream flowers, which open from red buds in late summer–autumn.

Species, variety or cultivar:
  –
Other common names:
  Red-Hot Poker, Torch Lily
Height and spread:
  1.2 x 0.5 m (48 x 20 in)
Blooming period:
  Summer to autumn
Soil type:
  Moist, humus-rich, well-drained soil
Sun or Shade:
  Prefers full to part-sun
Hardiness:
  Minimum temp –18°C (0°F)

Kniphofia northiae • *Red-Hot Poker*

DESCRIPTION

There are nearly 70 species in this genus in the asphodel (Asphodelaceae) family, almost all from South Africa, which are clump-forming perennials with grassy to sword-shaped, often evergreen foliage emerging from vigorous rhizomes. They make excellent cut flowers and many hybrids and cultivars have been raised, in a variety of sizes and flower colours. Named after German professor Johann Hieronymus Kniphof (1704–1763).

K. northiae is an evergreen species with thick, broad, slightly blue-green leaves with a deep central keel, and dense cylindrical heads of pale yellow flowers that open from red buds in late spring–autumn.

Species, variety or cultivar:
–
Other common names:
Red-Hot Poker, Torch Lily
Height and spread:
1.5 x 0.1 m (60 x 40 in)
Blooming period:
Spring to autumn
Soil type:
Moist, humus-rich, well-drained soil
Sun or Shade:
Likes full to part-sun
Hardiness:
Minimum temp –12°C (10°F)

Kniphofia triangularis • *Red-Hot Poker*

DESCRIPTION

This mainly South African genus was named after German professor Johann Hieronymus Kniphof (1704–1763), and they are grown for their mainly autumn to spring spikes of intensely coloured, usually orange and/or yellow, flowers, borne in bottlebrush heads at the top of strong, tall, upright stems. Many hybrids and cultivars have been raised, in a variety of sizes and flower colours.

K. triangularis is an evergreen, with narrow grassy foliage and fairly narrow flower stems with small heads of orange-pink to soft red flowers, which appear from late summer. Plant in an open, sunny position in moist, humus-rich, well-drained soil.

Species, variety or cultivar:
  –
Other common names:
  Red-Hot Poker, Torch Lily
Height and spread:
  90 x 60 cm (36 x 24 in)
Blooming period:
  Summer
Soil type:
  Moist, humus-rich, well-drained soil
Sun or Shade:
  Enjoys both full and part-sun
Hardiness:
  Minimum temp –12°C (10°F)

Kniphofia • *Red-Hot Poker*

DESCRIPTION

Most of the nearly 70 species in this genus are South African, clump-forming perennials with grassy to sword-shaped, often evergreen foliage that emerges from vigorous rhizomes. They make excellent cut flowers, and many hybrids and cultivars have been raised, in a variety of sizes and flower colours. A popular and attractive hybrid is 'Primrose Beauty', which has fine grassy foliage, and bright yellow flowers on 60 cm (24 in) stems.

Hardiness varies, though none will tolerate repeated heavy frosts. Plant in an open, sunny position in moist, humus-rich, well-drained soil. Water and feed well during active growth. Most will tolerate salt winds and thrive near the coast.

Species, variety or cultivar:
    hybrid cultivar, 'Primrose Beauty'
Other common names:
    Red-Hot Poker, Torch Lily
Height and spread:
    60 x 50 cm (24 x 20 in)
Blooming period:
    Autumn to spring
Soil type:
    Moist, humus-rich, well-drained soil
Sun or Shade:
    Likes full sun and part-shade
Hardiness:
    Minimum temp −12°C (10°F)

Lamium maculatum • *Dead Nettle*

DESCRIPTION

This genus of about 50 species of low-growing annuals and perennials, which often spread by rhizomes or runners, occurs naturally in Europe, North Africa and temperate Asia, but some are also widely naturalized elsewhere and have become weeds.

From Europe, western Asia and North Africa, *L. maculatum* is a spreading, sometimes mounding or scrambling, near-evergreen perennial. The stems are long, rooting as they spread, with downy, toothed, pointed oval to triangular, often white-marked leaves, to over 8 cm (3 in) long. Heads of up to eight widely spaced pinkish red to purple, rarely white, flowers, to 18 mm (¾ in) long, appear in summer.

Species, variety or cultivar:
–

Other common names:
Dead Nettle

Height and spread:
50 x 150 cm (20 x 60 in)

Blooming period:
Spring

Soil type:
Moist, humus-rich, well-drained soil

Sun or Shade:
Likes a partly-shaded or shaded position

Hardiness:
Minimum temp –34°C (–30°F)

Lantana camara • *Lantana*

DESCRIPTION

A small genus of about 150 species, these plants are mostly found in tropical America. They have scrambling, somewhat prickly stems, simple opposite leaves, rough on both surfaces, and small flowers grouped in dense flattened or hemispherical heads, with the youngest flowers at the centre.

L. camara is an evergreen shrub from the West Indies and Central America, which flowers in shades ranging from creamy white through yellow, orange and pink to brick red, the heads often appearing bicoloured owing to florets ageing to another colour. Wild forms are particularly invasive colonizers, proclaimed as noxious weeds in some warm-climate countries. 'Orange Carpet' has a trailing habit, and orange flowers.

Species, variety or cultivar:
'Orange Carpet'
Other common names:
Lantana
Height and spread:
3.5 x 9 m (12 x 30 ft)
Blooming period:
All year
Soil type:
Light, fertile soils with free drainage
Sun or Shade:
Likes full sun
Hardiness:
Minimum temp −7°C (20°F)

Lathyrus grandiflorus • *Everlasting Pea*

DESCRIPTION

This genus of 110 species of annuals and
perennials is found in Eurasia, North America,
temperate South America and the mountains
of East Africa; many are climbers, others are
low-spreading plants and some are shrubby.
The flowers are typically pea-like, occurring in
many colours, and may be solitary or in
racemes arising from the upper leaf axils.

L. *grandiflorus* is found from Sicily to the
southern Balkans, and is a climbing perennial
with angled stems, tendril-tipped leaves and
paired 5 cm (2 in) long leaflets. Sprays of up
to four violet and pink flowers, 30 mm (1¼ in)
across, are borne in summer.

Species, variety or cultivar:
 –
Other common names:
 Everlasting Pea, Two-Flowered Pea
Height and spread:
 2 x 2 m (7 x 7 ft)
Blooming period:
 Summer
Soil type:
 Moist, well-drained soil
Sun or Shade:
 Enjoys full sun
Hardiness:
 Minimum temp –23°C (–10°F)

Lathyrus vernus • *Spring Vetch*

DESCRIPTION

This genus is comprised of 110 species of annuals and perennials found in Eurasia, North America, temperate South America and the mountains of East Africa. Plant in moist well-drained soil and provide stakes or wires for climbers.

L. vernalis is an often semi-evergreen perennial from Europe, which has angular stems, and leaves with one to two pairs of leaflets to 10 cm (4 in) long. Long racemes of up to 15 flowers, 18 mm (¾ in) across, initially purple-red, but ageing to blue-green, appear in early spring. 'Rosenelfe' is a 30 cm (12 in) tall cultivar, with pale pink flowers.

Species, variety or cultivar:
  'Rosenelfe'
Other common names:
  Spring Vetch
Height and spread:
  30 x 50 cm (12 x 20 in)
Blooming period:
  Spring
Soil type:
  Moist, well-drained soil
Sun or Shade:
  Likes full sun
Hardiness:
  Minimum temp –34°C (–30°F)

Leontopodium alpinum • *Edelweiss*

DESCRIPTION

A rock garden favourite, Leontopodium is a member of the daisy (Asteraceae) family. The approximately 60 species that make up this genus are hardy, herbaceous, alpine perennials. Most are native to mountain regions of east and central Asia, with only one species occurring in Europe.

L. alpinum is the only European species, and is a creeping short-lived perennial growing wild in the Alps, Carpathians and Pyrenees. The woolly silvery-grey leaves are 5–8 cm (2–3 in) long, and star-shaped white flowers with a central yellow floret surrounded by long floral bracts appear in early summer in alpine meadows, on scree slopes and among rocks.

Species, variety or cultivar:
–

Other common names:
Edelweiss

Height and spread:
15 x 22 cm (6 x 9 in)

Blooming period:
Summer

Soil type:
Well-drained, gritty or sandy soil

Sun or Shade:
Enjoys full sun

Hardiness:
Minimum temp –34°C (–30°F)

Lewisia cotyledon • *Bitter Root*

DESCRIPTION

This species, one of 19 in the genus, is from the area around the California–Oregon State line, and is an evergreen with loose rosettes of spatula-shaped leaves, with edges often wavy, rarely toothed. Panicles of starry 7- to 10-petalled flowers are borne at the ends of short wiry stems from mid-spring to early summer. Wild plants have purple-pink flowers; natural varieties and cultivars come in many shades. 'White Splendour' has dark green foliage and pure white flowers. The genus was named after North American explorer Captain Meriwether Lewis (1774–1809) of the famed Lewis and Clark expedition of 1806–7.

Species, variety or cultivar:
'White Splendour'

Other common names:
Bitter root

Height and spread:
30 x 20 cm (12 x 8 in)

Blooming period:
Spring

Soil type:
Gritty, free-draining soil, moist during the growing season, but otherwise dry

Sun or Shade:
Likes both part-sun and full sun

Hardiness:
Minimum temp –29°C (20°F)

Liatris spicata • *Blazing Star*

DESCRIPTION

Native to eastern North America, the 35 species of perennials in this genus of the daisy (Asteraceae) family make a bold splash of colour in summer and couldn't be easier to grow. Native Americans used the roots medicinally, and early settlers found that the dried roots repelled clothes moths. While hardiness varies, most species are frost resistant. Wild plants are usually found along watercourses, though they can be grown in any sunny position in moist, humus-rich, well-drained soil. Locate at the back of borders to disguise the foliage clump and make use of the flower stem's height.

Found across most of eastern USA, *L. spicata* has an upright habit and narrow, sometimes linear leaves, to 20 cm (8 in) long. In mid-summer to autumn, dense spikes of purple-red flowerheads, to 60 cm (24 in) long, are borne. 'Callilepsis Purple' is a 60 cm (24 in) high cultivar, with dark purple flowerheads.

RIGHT: The *Liatris spicata* will tend to develop mildew if it has insufficient sunlight and air circulation, so be sure to give it plenty of room. This plant may be started from seeds sown indoors at 65-75 degrees or directly into the garden in early spring, but they will not bloom until their second year. Germination takes from 20 to 45 days.

Species, variety or cultivar:
  'Callilepsis Purple'
Other common names:
  Blazing Star, Button Snake Root, Gayfeather
Height and spread:
  60 x 30 cm (24 x 12 in)
Blooming period:
  Summer to autumn
Soil type:
  Moist, humus-rich, well-drained soil
Sun or Shade:
  Likes full or part-sun
Hardiness:
  Minimum temp –40°C (–40°F)

Libertia formosa • *Showy Libertia*

DESCRIPTION

The nine species of perennial rhizomatous plants in this genus, a Southern Hemisphere member of the iris (Iridaceae) family, have a creeping or tufted growth habit and a prolonged flowering season. They occur in eastern Australia, New Zealand, New Guinea and the Andes of South America. The strap-like leaves are produced in sparse to dense tufts. The flowers, usually white and recognizably iris-like in form, are borne in clusters at the top of straight stems.

L. *formosa* is a clumping perennial from Chile with narrow, strap-shaped, leathery, dark green leaves and tall spikes of white or pale yellow flowers in late spring.

Species, variety or cultivar:
–
Other common names:
Showy Libertia, Snowy Mermaid
Height and spread:
90 x 60 cm (36 x 24 in)
Blooming period:
Spring
Soil type:
Tolerant of poor soils
Sun or Shade:
Prefers full sun
Hardiness:
Minimum temp –7°C (20°F)

Ligularia przewalskii • *Shavalski's Ligularia*

DESCRIPTION

There are some 125 species of perennials in Ligularia. In spring these vigorous plants soon develop into clumps of long-stalked, broad, basal leaves, usually kidney- to heart-shaped, with toothed edges. In summer and autumn flowering stems develop, ranging from broadly forking panicles of large yellow to orange daisies, to tall spike-like racemes of numerous smaller heads, depending on the species.

L. przewalskii is a vigorous perennial from northern China, with deeply palmately lobed and toothed, basal leaves to 30 cm (12 in) long and wide. The stems are a dark purple-red, and narrow spikes of many spidery golden yellow flowerheads appear in summer and autumn.

Species, variety or cultivar:
–

Other common names:
Shavalski's Ligularia

Height and spread:
2 x 0.12 m (7 x 4 ft)

Blooming period:
Summer to autumn

Soil type:
Deep, fertile, humus-rich soil, kept moist through the year

Sun or Shade:
Full or part-sun

Hardiness:
Minimum temp –34°C (–30°F)

Linum doerfleri • *Flax*

DESCRIPTION

This genus, which includes the important fibre and oilseed plant flax, *L. usitatissum*, and which gives its name to the family Linaceae, comprises about 180 species, native to temperate or subtropical regions of the world though predominantly from the Northern Hemisphere. They are delicate but easy-to-grow plants. The stems are erect and branching, and the grey-green leaves are simple and narrow. Cup-shaped to funnel-shaped 5-petalled flowers are carried in branched clusters at the stem tips, lasting only one day. Colours vary with the variety but are mostly shades of blue or yellow, less commonly red, pink or white, and they are produced in great numbers throughout the summer.

L. doerfleri is a compact mat-forming perennial, with small, oval, pointed, dull green leaves, and is endemic to Crete, Greece. Solitary, bright yellow, star-shaped flowers are borne in the upper leaf axils in spring, and this species makes an ideal rock garden plant.

BELOW: The use of flax for weaving into 'linen' cloth dates back to Egyptian dynasties over 4,000 years ago and from the latter part of the Middle Ages it became the most commonly used textile material in Europe. It was not until the early part of the nineteenth century that cotton began to challenge this premier position. Today flax is also widely grown for its oil-yielding seed.

Species, variety or cultivar:

–

Other common names:

Flax

Height and spread:

8 x 30 cm (3 x 12 in)

Blooming period:

Spring

Soil type:

Well-drained humus-rich soil

Sun or Shade:

Needs full sun

Hardiness:

Minimum temp –12°C (10°F)

Liriope muscari • *Lily Turf*

DESCRIPTION

This small genus comprises five or six species of evergreen or semi-evergreen frost-hardy perennials that come from acid-soil woodland habitats in East Asia. Tough, mat-forming and more or less trouble-free plants, they are used in gardens to add structure, defeat weeds and edge shrubberies.

From China, Taiwan and Japan, *L. muscari* is a drought-tolerant, tough, sturdy, evergreen, spreading ground cover. The leaves are narrow, grass-like, glossy deep green and mat-forming, and dense, bead-like, steely deep lavender flowers, held on blunt spikes, appear in late autumn. 'Monroe White' has numerous white flowers and requires full shade.

Species, variety or cultivar:
'Monroe White'

Other common names:
Lily Turf

Height and spread:
30 x 45 cm (12 x 18 in)

Blooming period:
Autumn

Soil type:
Well-drained, sandy soil

Sun or Shade:
Likes full shade

Hardiness:
Minimum temp–34°C (–30°F)

Lobelia cardinalis • *Cardinal Flower*

DESCRIPTION

The cultivated lobelias are mainly perennials from the Americas, most of which form a basal clump of simple leaves, from which emerge upright flower stems bearing spikes of

tubular 5-lobed flowers, the lower three lobes enlarged. Native Americans used lobelia species medicinally and the Cherokee of the eighteenth century reputedly had an infallible lobelia-based cure for syphilis.

L. cardinalis, from North America, is a short-lived perennial that forms a clump of upright stems with often red-tinted, narrow, pointed oval to lance-shaped leaves, to 10 cm (4 in) long. Long spikes of bright red flowers, to over 25 mm (1 in) wide, appear in summer to autumn.

Species, variety or cultivar:
  –
Other common names:
  Cardinal Flower
Height and spread:
  90 x 40 cm (36 x 16 in)
Blooming period:
  Summer to autumn
Soil type:
  Moist, well-drained soil
Sun or Shade:
  Prefers a sunny position, but can
  cope with part-shade
Hardiness:
  Minimum temp –40°C (–40°F)

Lotus berthelotii • *Parrot's Beak*

DESCRIPTION

A genus of about 150 species found almost worldwide in open grasslands and rocky places, all but a few species native to temperate regions of the Northern Hemisphere. The leaves are small and pinnate, often with only four or five leaflets, and sometimes closely hairy, giving them a silvery appearance. The pea-like flowers come in a range of colours, from white to yellow, pink or red, and are borne singly or in clusters in the leaf axils. The most colourful are several large-flowered species from the Canary Islands and Madeira, with yellow or red flowers adapted to pollination by birds. Popular in garden borders, the trailing types are well suited to hanging baskets or pots.

L. berthelotii is from the Canary Islands and is a popular, trailing, evergreen plant, which has silvery grey leaves, with needle-like leaflets. Red flowers with black centres, 35 mm (1½ in) long, are borne in spring to summer.

BELOW: From late spring to early summer the blooms are freely produced in pairs, usually deep red or scarlet, and resembling a parrot's beak, hence the comical common name. It is

suitable for growing in hanging baskets and over the sides of containers. However, it is not hardy and needs to be moved to a frost-free place during winter.

Species, variety or cultivar:
–

Other common names:
Coral Gem, Parrot's Beak, Pelican's Beak

Height and spread:
0.02 x 1.8 m (8 x 72 in)

Blooming period:
Spring to summer

Soil type:
Well-drained soil

Sun or Shade:
Likes full sun

Hardiness:
Minimum temp −1°C (30°F)

Lupinus • *Lily Turf*

DESCRIPTION

There are about 200 species of annuals, perennials and evergreen shrubs in this genus, which is a member of the pea-flower subfamily of legumes. They are found in North and South America, southern Europe and northern Africa, usually in dry habitats.

Perennial lupins were first hybridized in the 1890s, but gained most popularity with the hybrids George Russell developed between 1911 and 1937. Known as the Russell lupins, these laid the foundations for later cultivars of hybrid lupins. Many of these later perennial hybrids are still informally referred to as Russell lupins. 'Queen of Hearts' has scarlet and creamy yellow bicolour flowers.

Species, variety or cultivar:
  hybrid cultivar, Russell lupin,
  'Queen of Hearts'
Other common names:
  Lupin, Lupine
Height and spread:
  1.2 x 1.5 m (4 x 5 ft)
Blooming period:
  Summer
Soil type:
  Moderately fertile, well-
  drained soil
Sun or Shade:
  Best in full sun
Hardiness:
  Minimum temp –40°C (–40°F)

Lychnis coronaria • *Dusty Miller*

DESCRIPTION

Lychnis or lukhnis is a Greek word meaning 'lamp', and this genus of 20 species was given its name in the third century BC by Theophrastus, presumably because of its vivid flowerheads. Found in the northern temperate zone, Lychnis species are quite variable, often forming large clumps of foliage, sometimes with silver-grey leaves.

L. coronaria has a spreading mounding habit and is from southeastern Europe. The leaves are lance-shaped, to about 8 cm (3 in) long, often smaller and covered with dense silver-grey hairs, as are the stems. Small heads of flowers, usually in vivid shades of pink or purple-red, appear in summer. The cultivar 'Alba' has white flowers.

Species, variety or cultivar:
'Alba'

Other common names:
Dusty Miller, Rose Campion

Height and spread:
80 x 100 cm (32 x 40 in)

Blooming period:
Summer

Soil type:
Moist, well-drained soil

Sun or Shade:
Easily grown in sun or part-shade

Hardiness:
Minimum temp –34°C (–30°F)

Lysichiton americanus • *Yellow Skunk Cabbage*

Description

The two species in this genus in the arum (Araceae) family grow in bogs in northeast Asia and western North America. They have large paddle-shaped leaves, preceded in spring by almost stemless arum-type flowers of yellow or white. These are followed in summer by spikes of green-skinned fruit. The common name, which alludes to the musky smell of the leaves when crushed, is a complete overstatement.

L. americanus is from western North America, is the larger of the two species and is found in swamps and bogs. Flowers with a bright yellow spathe, rising to 40 cm (16 in), appear in early spring, followed by tall, bright green, paddle-shaped leaves.

Species, variety or cultivar:
–
Other common names:
Yellow Skunk Cabbage
Height and spread:
1.2 x 1.5 m (4 x 5 ft)
Blooming period:
Spring
Soil type:
Damp to wet, humus-rich mud
Sun or Shade:
Likes sun or semi-shade
Hardiness:
Minimum temp –23°C (–10°F)

Lysimachia congestiflora • *Loosestrife*

DESCRIPTION

The genus name Lysimachia has a long history: Dioscorides, a physician in Nero's army, allegedly named yellow loosestrife after King Lysimachus of Thrace. Belonging to the primrose (Primulaceae) family, this genus of about 150 species is found not only in Thrace (northern Greece) but also over much of Europe and Asia, as well as in North America and South Africa.

L. *congestiflora*, from temperate East Asia, is a perennial that forms a densely foliaged mound of dark green, often red-tinted, pointed oval leaves, topped with clusters of golden yellow flowers in late spring. 'Outback Sunset' has yellow-green leaves with a darker central zone.

Species, variety or cultivar:
  'Outback Sunset'
Other common names:
  Loosestrife
Height and spread:
  15 x 40 cm (6 x 16 in)
Blooming period:
  Summer
Soil type:
  Moist, well-drained garden soil
Sun or Shade:
  Perfectly happy in full sun or half-sun
Hardiness:
  Minimum temp–34°C (–30°F)

Lythrum salicaria • *Purple Loosestrife*

DESCRIPTION

This genus of about 35 species is a member of the loosestrife (Lythraceae) family. The flowers are small, rather star-shaped and carried in racemes. They make attractive cut flowers and are at home in the border. The name Lythrum is derived from the Greek lythron, meaning 'blood', referring to the colour of the flowers.

L. *salicaria* is from temperate Eurasia, Africa and Australia, but is widely naturalized in North America, where it is regarded as a bad weed. It has mid-green leaves and spikes, 22–30 cm (9–12 in) long, of small red-purple flowers which appear in early summer to early autumn. 'Robert' has bright cerise pink flowers.

Species, variety or cultivar:
'Robert'
Other common names:
Purple Loosestrife, Striped Loosestrife
Height and spread:
150 x 60 cm (60 x 24 in)
Blooming period:
Summer to autumn
Soil type:
Ordinary garden soil
Sun or Shade:
Enjoys full sun or half-sun
Hardiness:
Minimum temp –40°C (–40°F)

Macleaya microcarpa • *Plume Poppy*

DESCRIPTION

This genus includes two species of hardy herbaceous perennials, sometimes sold under the name Bocconia. They have scalloped, deeply lobed, heart-shaped, grey to olive green leaves, 15–20 cm (6–8 in) long, similar to fig leaves. The genus is named after Alexander Macleay, former secretary of the Linnean Society of London.

M. *microcarpa* is from central China, with downy leaves that are greyish green to olive with white undersides. Tiny flowers, which are pink outside and bronze inside, are borne in large plume-like panicles, 30 cm (12 in) long, in autumn. Care should be taken, as this species can be very invasive.

Species, variety or cultivar:
—

Other common names:
Plume Poppy

Height and spread:
2.4 x 0.9 m (8 x 3 ft)

Blooming period:
Autumn

Soil type:
Deep, loamy soil

Sun or Shade:
Likes a sheltered sunny position

Hardiness:
Minimum temp −40°C (−40°F)

Malva moschata • *Musk Mallow*

DESCRIPTION

This genus contains at least 30 species of annuals, biennials and short-lived herbaceous perennials that are similar to hollyhocks, but are bushier and have smaller leaves. These easily cultivated plants are native to Europe, North Africa and Asia. Like the hollyhock, to which it is related, Malva is a member of the mallow (Malvaceae) family, and its flowers occur in shades of white, pink, blue or purple. Ideal for herbaceous or annual borders, they do best in a sunny position but will tolerate partial shade in well-drained soil.

M. moschata is a European perennial with narrow, finely cut, mid-green leaves that give off a musky smell when brushed or crushed. Abundant, saucer-shaped, rose-pink flowers are borne in summer. 'Alba' has attractive single, white, 5-petalled flowers and a bushy branching habit. Remove spent flowers to encourage a second flowering, and cut down to the ground in autumn. Propagate from cuttings or seed in spring.

LEFT: If you cut the musk mallow back to the ground when the flowering is almost over in the summer then you will generally be rewarded with a fresh flush of flowers in late summer.

Species, variety or cultivar:
'Alba'
Other common names:
Musk Mallow
Height and spread:
100 x 45 cm (40 x 18 in)
Blooming period:
Summer
Soil type:
Well-drained soil
Sun or Shade:
Does best in a sunny position, but will tolerate partial shade
Hardiness:
Minimum temp –40°C (–40°F)

Malva sylvestris • *Common Mallow*

DESCRIPTION

Like the hollyhock, to which it is related, Malva is a member of the mallow (Malvaceae) family. The roughly 30 species are native to Europe, North Africa and Asia, and are well suited for herbaceous or annual borders. They do best in a sunny position but will tolerate partial shade in well-drained soil.

M. sylvestris is a biennial or perennial from Europe, with alternate green leaves to 10 cm (4 in) long. The 5-petalled single flowers are rose-purple with dark veins, and are borne in early summer to early autumn or until frosts. 'Primley Blue' has bluish purple flowers with dark blue veins.

Species, variety or cultivar:
'Primley Blue'
Other common names:
Cheeses, Common Mallow, High Mallow
Height and spread:
0.9 x 8 m (3 x 25 ft)
Blooming period:
Summer
Soil type:
Well-drained soil
Sun or Shade:
Prefers a sunny position, but copes with partial shade
Hardiness:
Minimum temp –40°C (–40°F)

Matthiola incana • *Brompton Stock*

DESCRIPTION

The 55 mainly temperate Eurasian species of this genus are famed for their scent. Stocks were once grown for medicinal purposes and a comment attributed to Italian botanist Pierandrea Mattioli, after whom the genus is named, that he grew stock only for 'matters of love and lust,' suggests the medicine had much to do with the scent.

M. *incana* is from southern and western Europe and has elliptical, grey-green, downy leaves, 5 cm (2 in) long. Upright spikes of scented purple, pink or white flowers appear in summer. The Vintage Series grows to 15–20 cm (6–8 in), is branching and occurs in most colours, such as 'Vintage Lilac'.

Species, variety or cultivar:
'Vintage Lilac'
Other common names:
Brompton Stock
Height and spread:
80 x 30 cm (32 x 12 in)
Blooming period:
Summer
Soil type:
Moist, well-drained soil
Sun or Shade:
Likes full sun
Hardiness:
Minimum temp –12°C (10°F)

Meconopsis grandis • *Blue Poppy*

DESCRIPTION

Mainly native to the Himalayan region, this genus of over 40 species from the poppy (Papaveraceae) family is known for its blue-flowered species, but the other more traditional poppies of yellow, pink or red are often more easily grown. Most species grow best in woodland conditions in a cool-temperate climate with reliable rainfall.

M. grandis is a Himalayan perennial, with foliage and stems that have rusty brown hairs. The lower leaves grow to 30 cm (12 in) long, are elliptical, and serrated to coarsely toothed. Long-stemmed deep blue to purple-blue flowers, in groups of three or more, are borne from late spring to early summer.

Species, variety or cultivar:
  –
Other common names:
  Asiatic Poppy, Blue Poppy, Indian Poppy
Height and spread:
  1.2 x 0.6 m (48 x 24 in)
Blooming period:
  Summer
Soil type:
  Moist, deep, humus-rich, well-drained soil
Sun or Shade:
  Likes a sheltered, part-shaded position
Hardiness:
  Minimum temp –29°C (–20°F)

Mimulus cardinalis • *Scarlet Monkey Flower*

DESCRIPTION

There are some 180 species in this mostly American genus of vigorous upright plants. Stems are covered in fine hairs and sticky glands, which may also be present on the leaves, and flowers form in the leaf axils. The annuals and perennials often have flowers with vividly contrasting colour patterns, but this is less common among the shrubs.

M. cardinalis is a vigorous clumping perennial from southern North America, which roots down when a stem touches ground. The stems are sticky, and the leaves are to 12 cm (5 in) long. Scarlet tubular flowers, borne in the leaf axils, appear in summer.

Species, variety or cultivar:
   –
Other common names:
   Scarlet Monkey Flower
Height and spread:
   90 x 70 cm (36 x 27 in)
Blooming period:
   Spring to summer
Soil type:
   Well-drained soil kept
   moist during summer
Sun or Shade:
   Likes full sun
Hardiness:
   Minimum temp –18°C (0°F)

Miscanthus sinensis • *Eulalia*

DESCRIPTION

This genus contains about 20 species from Africa to East Asia, and these tufted spreading plants have showy, green, silver, white and mottled foliage. The flowers are ideal for floral work as they dry well and hold their form for months. Bright autumn tonings, from orange, red, yellow or purples, may appear.

M. sinensis is a tall clump-forming grass from Japan and China with blue-green leaves that turn vivid orange–reds and yellows in autumn. Support should be given in windy areas and flower spikes from silver-pink to reddish purple, appear in autumn. 'Variegatus' (variegated Japanese silver grass), has loose, pendulous, green and white-striped foliage.

Species, variety or cultivar:
  'Variegatus'
Other common names:
  Eulalia, Japanese Silver Grass
Height and spread:
  4.5 x 1.2 m (15 x 4 ft)
Blooming period:
  Autumn
Soil type:
  Moist open soils
Sun or Shade:
  Prefers full sun
Hardiness:
  Minimum temp –29°C (–20°F)

Monarda • *Bergamot*

DESCRIPTION

This genus, named after Nicholas Monardes (1493–1588), a Spanish botanist, once physician to Phillip II, is a member of the mint (Lamiaceae) family and contains 16 species of annuals and perennials from North America. In summer the top of each stem carries several whorls of tubular flowers backed by leafy bracts. The origin of the common name bee balm is obvious on any sunny day in summer, when bees continuously visit the flowers.

The two most commonly grown species, *M. didyma* and *M. fistulosa*, hybridize freely resulting in excellent garden varieties such as 'Cambridge Scarlet', which has large ruby red flowers.

Species, variety or cultivar:
 hybrid cultivar, 'Cambridge Scarlet'
Other common names:
 Bee Balm, Bergamot, Horsemint
Height and spread:
 150 x 80 cm (60 x 32 in)
Blooming period:
 Summer
Soil type:
 Moist, well-drained soils
Sun or Shade:
 Enjoys an open sunny position
Hardiness:
 Minimum temp –34°C (–30°F)

Moraea villosa • *Peacock Iris*

DESCRIPTION

Belonging to the iris (Iridaceae) family, this genus consists of about 120 species of which only a few are commonly cultivated, and originates in sub-Saharan Africa from Ethiopia to South Africa where they are found in moist grasslands. The short-lived, iris-like, clustered flowers, often in brilliant colours, are produced in succession during spring and early summer. In garden conditions a dry dormancy period in summer is essential, as is very sharp drainage. However, when these conditions are met, the plants withstand more frost than their native habitats would suggest. They are super tough in conditions of winter wet.

Species, variety or cultivar:
–
Other common names:
Peacock Iris
Height and spread:
40 x 12 cm (16 x 5 in)
Blooming period:
Spring
Soil type:
Well-drained soil
Sun or Shade:
Likes full sun
Hardiness:
Minimum temp –7°C (20°F)

The striking *M. villosa* is from Western Cape, South Africa, but is rare in the wild. Flat white to orange or blue flowers, up to 8 cm (3 in) wide, with large, deep blue, circular blotches at the base of each of three petals, appear in late winter to early spring. Propagate from seed, sowing in autumn.

LEFT: *Moraea villosa* has three, broad, rounded petals (and three very narrow ones as well) in shades including blue, yellow, orange and cream, but each with a rounded splash of glowing peacock-blue or green exactly like the eye on a peacock's tail and with the same sheen. A lovely pot or window-box plant.

Morina longifolia • *Whorlflower*

DESCRIPTION

This genus has four species of prickly-leafed evergreen perennials that are native to eastern Europe and Asia. The leaves are mainly basal, through which they produce

upright spikes of curved tubular flowers in whorls supported by prickly green bracts. Grow in a sunny aspect in well-drained but moist soil and protect plants from winter wet.

M. longifolia is a rosette-forming perennial from the Himalayas, with spine-edged leaves to 25 cm (10 in) long. In summer an upright flower stem bears whorls of curved tubular flowers, to 30 mm (1¼ in) across, which are white, turning pink with age.

Species, variety or cultivar:
–
Other common names:
Whorlflower
Height and spread:
90 x 30 cm (36 x 12 in)
Blooming period:
Spring to summer
Soil type:
Well-drained but moist soil
Sun or Shade:
Likes a sunny aspect
Hardiness:
Minimum temp –23°C (–10°F)

Muscari latifolium • *Grape Hyacinth*

DESCRIPTION

Coming originally from the Mediterranean basin and southwest Asia, the roughly 30 species of this genus are widely used today in woodland gardens and for bedding displays worldwide. The flowers, like tiny upside-down bowls hanging in dense clusters from pole-like stems, appear in spring. The lower florets open before those at the top of the pile. The foliage is voluminous and sometimes untidy.

M. *latifolium* is a bulbous perennial from southwest Asia with mid-green lance-shaped leaves. The flowers are violet-black, in an extended urn shape with pinched mouths, and racemes are topped with paler sterile flowers, in early summer.

Species, variety or cultivar:
–

Other common names:
Grape Hyacinth

Height and spread:
20 x 5 cm (8 x 2 in)

Blooming period:
Summer

Soil type:
Feed with bone meal in spring

Sun or Shade:
Requires winter sun

Hardiness:
Minimum temp –23°C (–10°F)

Nelumbo nucifera • *Sacred Lotus*

DESCRIPTION

This genus of two species of aquatic perennials belongs to the self-named lotus (Nelumbonaceae) family. In warm subtropical climates, grow these in outdoor ponds; in cool-temperate climates, plant them in shallow water or in tubs. Plant the rhizomes in baskets or beds of heavy rich soil mix. Grow in calm water in full sun and propagate by division of rhizomes or from seed.

N. nucifera (syn. *Nelumbium nelumbo*) is found from Iran to Japan, and in Australia. The round, bluish green, wavy-edged leaves are borne umbrella-like on long prickly stalks, usually above the water. The showy, very fragrant, pink or white flowers, up to 30 cm (12 in) wide, are also borne on long stalks, often over 90 cm (36 in) tall, in summer. Flat-topped seed heads follow the flowers – the viability of the seeds extends to several hundred years. 'Mrs Perry D. Slocum' features deep pink flowers that age to creamy yellow.

Species, variety or cultivar:
'Mrs Perry D. Slocum'

Other common names:
Sacred Lotus

Height and spread:
2 x 2 m (7 x 7 ft)

Blooming period:
Summer

Soil type:
Heavy rich soil

Sun or Shade:
Enjoys full sun

Hardiness:
Minimum temp –7°C (20°F)

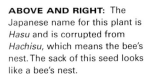

ABOVE AND RIGHT: The Japanese name for this plant is *Hasu* and is corrupted from *Hachisu*, which means the bee's nest. The sack of this seed looks like a bee's nest.

Nemesia denticulata

DESCRIPTION

This genus is a member of the figwort
(Scrophulariaceae) family and includes around 65
species of annuals, perennials and subshrubs,
confined to South Africa. They form small mounds
of toothed linear to lance-shaped foliage, and bear
clusters of flowers on short stems.

N. *denticulata* is a rather brittle-stemmed
mounding perennial with small bright green leaves.
The pleasantly scented dusky pink flowers are
produced in late spring to summer. Pinch back
when young to keep compact. This is a neat plant
for borders, rockeries or pots. Propagate from seed
in late autumn or early spring or grow from
cuttings of non-flowering stems.

Species, variety or cultivar:
–

Other common names:
–

Height and spread:
30 x 50 cm (12 x 20 in)

Blooming period:
Late spring to summer

Soil type:
Light, free-draining soil

Sun or Shade:
Prefers full sun to part-shade

Hardiness:
Minimum temp –12°C (10°F)

Nepeta x faassenii • *Catmint*

DESCRIPTION

A member of the mint (Lamiaceae) family, this genus contains around 250 mainly temperate Eurasian and North African aromatic perennials. It is represented in cultivation by just a few species, and one widely grown hybrid group. They are prized for the hazy effect created by their grey-green foliage and mauve-blue to purple flowerheads.

An often sprawling hybrid, *N. x faassenii* has grey-green to silver-grey, toothed, lance-shaped to pointed oval leaves. Throughout summer it produces numerous spikes of long-lasting lavender to deep purple-blue flowers. Propagate from seed or from cuttings of non-flowering stems. 'Six Hills Giant' features grey foliage and large sprays of lavender flowers.

Species, variety or cultivar:
  'Six Hills Giant'
Other common names:
  Catmint, Catnip
Height and spread:
  60 x 100 cm (24 x 40 in)
Blooming period:
  Summer
Soil type:
  Light, free-draining soil
Sun or Shade:
  Prefers full sun to part shade
Hardiness:
  Minimum temp –40°C (–40°F)

Nymphaea • *Waterlily*

DESCRIPTION

This genus, which belongs to the self-named
waterlily (Nymphaeaceae) family, is of varied
distribution, growing in ponds over most of the
world. It contains about 50 species of aquatic
perennials divided into hardy and tropical
groups. The hardy hybrids are suitable for
cooler climates. Their attractive flowers, in all
colours of the spectrum, are starry or globular,
with pointed or rounded petals of varying
number. They may be on stalks above the
foliage, or sit at water level. Some are
'changeables,' which alter their colouring
dramatically as they age.

'Colourado' bears attractive starry salmon
flowers, deepening in colour toward the centre.

Species, variety or cultivar:
hybrid cultivar, 'Colourado'
Other common names:
Waterlily
Height and spread:
38 x 240 cm (15 x 96 in)
Blooming period:
Spring to summer
Soil type:
Rich soil mix
Sun or Shade:
Enjoys full sun
Hardiness:
Minimum temp –40°C (–40°F)

Nymphaea • *Waterlily*

DESCRIPTION

Nymphaea hybrids are divided into hardy and tropical hybrids, with the tropical hybrids further divided into day- and night-blooming hybrids. Tropical Day-Blooming Hybrids need a water temperature of 21°C (70°F) and a winter temperature of 10°C (50°F).

These hybrids are available in all colours, including blue shades; some have flowers up to 38 cm (15 in) wide. The flowers are usually held above the foliage. These plants should be grown in full sun in undisturbed water. Overcrowded plants produce smaller flowers and the foliage lifts above the water. The attractive cultivar 'Star of Zanzibar' bears lovely rich purple-pink flowers held above the foliage on long stems.

Species, variety or cultivar:
  hybrid cultivar, 'Star of Zanzibar'
Other common names:
  Waterlily
Height and spread:
  38 x 350 cm (15 x 144 in)
Blooming period:
  Spring to summer
Soil type:
  Rich soil mix
Sun or Shade:
  Enjoys full sun
Hardiness:
  Minimum temp –40°C (40°F)

Oenothera • *Evening Primrose*

DESCRIPTION

This genus of over 120 species of annuals, biennials and perennials is found in the temperate zones of the Americas. Some have tap roots and tend to be upright, others have fibrous roots and a more sprawling habit. The common name reflects both the predominantly yellow flower colour and that many species open from evening or night, sometimes not lasting beyond the following morning.

'Lemon Sunset' is an erect hybrid perennial of uncertain parentage. It forms a mounding clump of small deep green leaves. Fragrant flowers, to 10 cm (4 in) wide, light yellow, ageing to deep pink or red, are borne in summer.

Species, variety or cultivar:
  hybrid cultivar, 'Lemon Sunset'
Other common names:
  Evening Primrose
Height and spread:
  100 x 80 cm (40 x 32 in)
Blooming period:
  Summer
Soil type:
  Light, gritty, free-draining soil
Sun or Shade:
  Prefers full sun
Hardiness:
  Minimum temp −29°C (−20°F)

Omphalodes cappadocica • *Navelwort*

DESCRIPTION

The 28-odd species of annuals, biennials and perennials in this genus are native to Europe, northern Africa, Asia and Mexico, where they grow in habitats such as shady rocks and cliffs, damp woodland or streamsides. The common and botanical names arise from the seed vessel's apparent resemblance to a navel.

O. *cappadocica* is a perennial, forming low clumps of heart-shaped leaves. Terminal clusters of small, blue, forget-me-not flowers, are borne in early to mid-summer. 'Cherry Ingram', is a taller vigorous form, with deeper blue flowers. Propagate from seed or by division, but care should be taken as it resents root disturbance.

Species, variety or cultivar:
  'Cherry Ingram'
Other common names:
  Navelwort
Height and spread:
  20 x 45 cm (8 x 18 in)
Blooming period:
  Early to mid-summer
Soil type:
  Moist, but well-drained soil
Sun or Shade:
  Likes shade
Hardiness:
  Minimum temp –23°C (–10°F)

Onosma alborosea

DESCRIPTION

This genus belongs to the borage (Boraginaceae) family and contains about 150 species of biennial and perennial herbs native to the Mediterranean and Asia. Closely related to comfrey (Symphytum), they are bristly plants, and are often woody based. The leaves are usually oblong and hairy or bristly to varying degrees. The tubular to bell-shaped flowers hang in clusters and are mostly yellow, blue or pink.

O. *alborosea* is a clump-forming perennial, native to southwestern Asia. The greyish green leaves are short, oblong and hairy. For long periods in summer, clusters of small hanging bellflowers are produced, in creamy white, ageing to pinkish purple.

Species, variety or cultivar:
–

Other common names:
–

Height and spread:
30 x 30 cm (12 x 12 in)

Blooming period:
Summer

Soil type:
Well-drained soil

Sun or Shade:
Prefers full sun

Hardiness:
Minimum temp –18°C (0°F)

Origanum vulgare • *Oregano*

DESCRIPTION

This genus, found from the Mediterranean region to East Asia, includes some of the best-known culinary herbs. Though consisting mostly of perennials, Origanum also includes a few subshrubs that have a tendency to become shrubby in mild climates, though they are often short lived.

A variable species found from Europe to Asia, *O. vulgare* is a popular culinary herb with very aromatic foliage. It has dark green oval to round leaves on 4-angled stems. The pink, purple or white flowers, usually with conspicuous bracts, are borne in spikes from summer to autumn.

Species, variety or cultivar:
–

Other common names:
Common Marjoram, Oregano, Wild Marjoram

Height and spread:
45 x 30 cm (18 x 12 in)

Blooming period:
Summer and autumn

Soil type:
Light, well-drained soil

Sun or Shade:
Prefers full sun

Hardiness:
Minimum temp –29°C (–20°F)

Osteospermum

DESCRIPTION

Mainly from southern Africa, this genus contains some 70 species of annuals, perennials and subshrubs. Mainly low, spreading or mounding plants, they have simple, broadly toothed, elliptical to spatula-shaped leaves. The flowers are large, with showy ray florets, mainly in pinks and purples, or white, and disc florets in an unusual purple-blue that contrasts with the golden anthers. The name comes from the Greek osteon, 'bone,' sperma, 'seed,' and refers to the hard seeds. Osteospermum species hybridize freely, especially in cultivation and new forms are constantly being introduced, such as 'Stardust', with deep pink ray florets. Propagate from tip cuttings.

Species, variety or cultivar:
hybrid cultivar, 'Stardust'
Other common names:
–
Height and spread:
30 x 60 cm (12 x 24 in)
Blooming period:
Summer, year-round in mild climates
Soil type:
Light, well-drained soil
Sun or Shade:
Likes full sun
Hardiness:
Minimum temp –7°C (20°F)

Pachysandra terminalis • *Japanese Spurge*

DESCRIPTION

Native to North America and East Asia, Pachysandra is a member of the box (Buxaceae) family and contains five species of low-growing shrubby or creeping perennials that spread by underground runners. Although slow to get started they are reliable once established. They are used for ground cover in shady places, and have the advantage of being able to grow over tree roots. The name Pachysandra comes from the Greek *pachys*, thick, and *andros*, man, referring to the thick stamens.

From Japan, *P. terminalis* features shiny dark green leaves with slightly toothed edges. Small white flowers are produced in spring.

Species, variety or cultivar:
–

Other common names:
Japanese Pachysandra, Japanese Spurge

Height and spread:
30 x 45 cm (12 x 18 in)

Blooming period:
Spring

Soil type:
Moist, slightly acidic soil, with organic matter incorporated

Sun or Shade:
Prefers shade

Hardiness:
Minimum temp –29°C (20°F)

Paeonia x lemoinei • *Peony*

DESCRIPTION

Mostly herbaceous perennials native to temperate parts of the Northern Hemisphere, this genus contains 30 or so species. These shrubby peonies, or tree peonies, have persistent woody stems, brilliantly coloured flowers and highly decorative foliage. Normally hardy, even in the coldest climates, they do need some protection from early spring frost.

P. x lemoinei is a group of cultivars originating as crosses between *P. lutea* and *P. suffruticosa*, inheriting the strong yellow colouring of *P. lutea*, usually flushed red in the centre or with the colours blended giving shades of orange. 'Roman Child' has semi-double yellow flowers with dark red blotches at the petal bases.

Species, variety or cultivar:
 'Roman Child'
Other common names:
 Peony
Height and spread:
 1.8 x 1.8 m (6 x 6 ft)
Blooming period:
 Spring to early summer
Soil type:
 Deep fertile soils of basaltic origin, heavily fed annually with organic matter
Sun or Shade:
 Does best in sun or part-shade
Hardiness:
 Minimum temp −23°C (−10°F)

Paeonia suffruticosa • *Tree Peony*

DESCRIPTION

Found from northwestern China and west to Bhutan, *P. suffruticosa* is a freely branching upright shrub. The smooth mid-green leaves are variously cut and lobed, and feature bluish green undersides. Solitary, large, sometimes double flowers are borne in mid-spring. They are white, pink, yellow or red, and have fluted petals that are frilled on the edges. The flowers of the many cultivars come in various shades of red, pink, white and violet, with a purplish blotch near the base; some are slightly fragrant. The cultivar 'Mountain Treasure' has white flowers, with a distinctive purplish blotch at the base of the petals.

Species, variety or cultivar:
'Mountain Treasure'

Other common names:
Moutan, Tree Peony

Height and spread:
2 x 2 m (7 x 7 ft)

Blooming period:
Mid-spring

Soil type:
Deep fertile soils of basaltic origin, heavily fed annually with organic matter

Sun or Shade:
Enjoys full sun to part-shade

Hardiness:
Minimum temp –34°C (–30°F)

Paeonia • *Peony*

DESCRIPTION

This genus of 30-odd species from temperate regions of the Northern Hemisphere belongs to the self-named peony (Paeoniaceae) family. The genus is named after Paeon, physician to the gods in Greek mythology. The breeding of herbaceous peonies was greatly enhanced by the introduction from China in the mid-eighteenth century of *P. lactiflora* (syn. *P. albiflora*), bringing, among other qualities, an attractive fragrance and the ability to produce double flowers. 'Buckeye Belle', one of the countless hybrid cultivars, has unusual semi-double, very dark red, rather crinkled petals and golden stamens.

These plants need protection from strong winds and scorching sun, but otherwise minimal maintenance is required to maintain shape and keep them looking good. Propagation from seed is not easy, as various special requirements have to be met; apical grafting is commonly used, with the graft union being buried 8 cm (3 in) below soil level.

BELOW: There is a myth that peonies need ants in order for blooms to open. In truth peonies develop a sugary coating on the flower buds, which ants and wasps enjoy, but the buds will open with or without these insects being present.

Species, variety or cultivar:
  hybrid cultivar, 'Buckeye Belle'
Other common names:
  Peony
Height and spread:
  90 x 90 cm (36 x 36 in)
Blooming period:
  Mid-spring
Soil type:
  Deep fertile soils of basaltic origin, heavily fed annually with organic matter
Sun or Shade:
  Enjoys full sun
Hardiness:
  Minimum temp –23°C (–10°F)

Papaver orientale • *Oriental Poppy*

DESCRIPTION

Among the most instantly recognized flowers, this widespread group of around 50 species of annuals and perennials gives its name to the poppy (Papaveraceae) family.

A western Asian perennial, *P. orientale* forms a sturdy clump of bristly, pinnate, often blue-green leaves that can be up to 25 cm (10 in) long. The flower stems are usually leafy on the lower half. Red, orange or pink, often darker blotched, solitary flowers, up to 10 cm (4 in) wide, are borne in summer. There are many cultivars, including 'Mrs Perry' with large salmon pink flowers. Propagate poppy cultivars from root cuttings, otherwise raise from seed.

Species, variety or cultivar:
  'Mrs Perry'
Other common names:
  Oriental Poppy
Height and spread:
  100 x 50 cm (40 x 20 in)
Blooming period:
  Summer
Soil type:
  Light, moist and well-drained soil
Sun or Shade:
  Likes full sun to part-shade
Hardiness:
  Minimum temp –40°C (–40°F)

Papaver rupifragum • *Poppy*

DESCRIPTION

Homer, the ninth-century BC Greek poet, first associated the hanging poppy bud with a dying soldier, and today poppies are synonymous with war remembrance days. Widely distributed, the 50-odd species in this genus form basal rosettes of usually finely lobed, often hairy leaves, while the flowers usually feature four crape-like petals around a central ovary topped with a prominent stigmatic disc.

Native to Spain, *P. rupifragum* is a perennial that forms a tufted clump of finely divided, downy, 10 cm (4 in) long leaves. Dusky light red-brown, solitary flowers to 8 cm (3 in) wide, occur in late spring to summer.

Species, variety or cultivar:
–
Other common names:
Poppy
Height and spread:
45 x 30 cm (18 x 12 in)
Blooming period:
Late spring to summer
Soil type:
Light, moist and well-drained soil
Sun or Shade:
Enjoys full sun to part-shade
Hardiness:
Minimum temp –18°C (0°F)

Pelargonium • *Storksbill*

DESCRIPTION

Most members of this genus come from South Africa, with a few from the rest of Africa, Australia and the Middle East. Pelargonium species interbreed freely and today there is a range of hybrid groups. This range includes: Angel Hybrids, Dwarf Hybrids, Regal Hybrids (also known as Martha Washington Hybrids), Scented-leafed Hybrids, Unique and Zonal Hybrids. These groups are mostly differentiated by stature, by flower type, or, in the case of Scented-leafed Hybrids, by their aromatic foliage. One such example of the Scented-leafed Hybrids is 'Gemstone' with attractive flowers in shades of pink to pinkish-red, with white blazes on the upper petals.

Species, variety or cultivar:
hybrid cultivar, 'Gemstone'
Other common names:
Storksbill
Height and spread:
75 x 100 cm (30 x 40 in)
Blooming period:
Spring to autumn
Soil type:
Light, well-drained soil
Sun or Shade:
Does best in full sun
Hardiness:
Minimum temp –7°C (20°F)

Penstemon digitalis • *Foxglove Beardtongue*

DESCRIPTION

This figwort family (Scrophulariaceae) genus of around 250 species of perennials and subshrubs is found from Alaska to Guatemala, with one straggler in cool-temperate Asia. Native Americans used parts of several species in herbal medicines, primarily for pain relief and to control bleeding.

P. digitalis is a summer-flowering perennial from central USA. The strongly upright stems are clothed in purple-tinted, glossy, 10–15 cm (4–6 in) long, blue-green leaves. The top 10–30 cm (4–12 in) of the stems is composed of panicles of white flowers that are flushed purple-pink. 'Husker Red' has deep purple-red foliage, especially on new growth.

Species, variety or cultivar:
  'Husker Red'
Other common names:
  Foxglove Beardtongue
Height and spread:
  1.5 x 0.6 m (5 x 2 ft)
Blooming period:
  Summer
Soil type:
  Moist, well-drained soil
Sun or Shade:
  Enjoys full sun to part-shade
Hardiness:
  Minimum temp –40°C (–40°F)

Petasites albus • *White Butterbur*

DESCRIPTION

This genus contains about 15 species of
herbaceous perennials from Europe, Asia and
North America in the daisy (Asteraceae) family.
They produce clusters or spikes of smallish
flowers, which are sometimes sweetly scented,
prior to the foliage – the kidney-shaped leaves
appear on upright stems in spring. They are good
ground covers in damp sites but some can
become quite invasive.

From north and central Europe and western
Asia, *P. albus* has 40 cm (16 in) wide leaves. The
yellow-white flowers, to 12 mm (½ in) across, are
borne in upright sprays in late winter. Propagate
by division while dormant.

Species, variety or cultivar:
–
Other common names:
White Butterbur
Height and spread:
40 x 200 cm (16 x 84 in)
Blooming period:
Late winter
Soil type:
Humus-rich moist to wet soil
Sun or Shade:
Prefers part-shade to full shade
Hardiness:
Minimum temp –29°C (–20°F)

Phalaris arundinacea • *Gardener's Garters*

DESCRIPTION

This genus contains around 15 species of both clumping annual and running perennial grasses that come from a wide range of habitats in North America, Asia, southern Africa and Europe.

P. arundinacea is a hardy perennial from Europe, Asia, southern Africa and North America. The soft arching leaves, to 35 cm (14 in) long, are borne on upright stems topped with soft fluffy flowerheads that start pale green and turn buff with maturity. This plant is usually only grown in one of its variegated forms, such as 'Picta', which has boldly white-striped leaves. Propagate by division.

Species, variety or cultivar:
'Picta'
Other common names:
Gardener's Garters, Reed Canary Grass, Ribbon Grass
Height and spread:
1.5 x 3 m (5 x 10 ft)
Blooming period:
Summer to autumn
Soil type:
Well-drained to moist soil
Sun or Shade:
Likes full sun to part-shade
Hardiness:
Minimum temp −34°C (−30°F)

Phlox paniculata • *Border Phlox*

DESCRIPTION

This North American genus of 67 annuals
and perennials belongs in the phlox
(Polemoniaceae) family. Phlox is Greek for
'flame,' a very appropriate term for the vivid
annual, rock, trailing and border types with
their fiery bursts of colour. While all types
share similar flowers, growth forms are
markedly different.

A vigorous eastern USA perennial, *P.
paniculata* forms thick clumps of upright
stems with pointed oval to lance-shaped
leaves that are often toothed, sometimes
downy. Borne in large rounded heads in
summer, the flowers are usually in pink,
lavender and purple shades. Propagate by
seed, division or cuttings.

Species, variety or cultivar:
–

Other common names:
Border Phlox, Perennial Phlox,
Summer Phlox

Height and spread:
120 x 100 cm (48 x 40 in)

Blooming period:
Summer

Soil type:
Well-drained soil that can be kept
moist

Sun or Shade:
Prefers full sun to part-shade

Hardiness:
Minimum temp –34°C (–30°F)

Phormium tenax • *New Zealand Flax*

DESCRIPTION

This genus of only two species of large evergreen perennials in the family Phormiaceae is restricted to New Zealand. *P. tenax* is a large impressive species with long, fibrous, upright leaves to 3 m (10 ft) long, usually grey-green in the wild forms. In summer it produces large candelabras of upright, waxy, red-brown trumpet-shaped flowers, which

are followed by decorative, shiny, black seed heads. 'Purpureum' has dark green leaves. The foliage was traditionally used to make cordage, and the dried seed heads are often used for decoration. Propagate from seed, or by division of the coloured leaf or dwarf clones in early spring.

Species, variety or cultivar:
'Purpureum'
Other common names:
New Zealand Flax, New Zealand Hemp
Height and spread:
4.5 x 3 m (15 x 10 ft)
Blooming period:
Summer
Soil type:
Moisture-retentive soil
Sun or Shade:
Likes full sun
Hardiness:
Minimum temp −12°C (10°F)

Phygelius aequalis

DESCRIPTION

There are just two species in this South African genus, which have been crossed to produce numerous hybrids, and which are often grown as herbaceous perennials where winters fall below freezing. In cold climates these plants need the protection of a wall or a similar warm spot to minimize frost damage. Propagate from cuttings taken in summer.

P. aequalis is a suckering shrub, or herbaceous perennial in colder climates. The soft bright green fleshy leaves are held on erect stems and hold pendent, fuchsia-like, dusky pink, tubular flowers during summer. 'Trewidden Pink' produces soft flesh pink flowers.

Species, variety or cultivar:
  'Trewidden Pink'
Other common names:
  –
Height and spread:
  0.9 x 0.9 m (3 x 3 ft)
Blooming period:
  Late summer
Soil type:
  Moist, humus-enriched, fertile soil
Sun or Shade:
  Prefers part-shade
Hardiness:
  Minimum temp –12°C (10°F)

Physalis philadelphica • *Jamberry*

DESCRIPTION

Widely distributed, especially in the Americas, but also in temperate Eurasia and Australia, this genus in the nightshade (Solanaceae) family consists of about 80 erect, bushy or sprawling annual and rhizomatous perennial herbs.

From Mexico and cultivated widely as a food crop, *P. philadelphica* (syns *P. ixocarpa, P. subglabrata*) has smooth-edged, toothed, oval to broadly sword-shaped leaves. The flowers feature open, yellow corollas marked with purplish brown and 5-lobed, bell-shaped, green calyces, veined with yellow, which enlarge to 5 cm (2 in) to enclose the yellow to purple edible berries. 'Purple de Milpa' has small, purple, sharp-tasting fruit.

Species, variety or cultivar:
  'Purple de Milpa'
Other common names:
  Jamberry, Miltomate, Purple Ground Cherry, Tomatillo
Height and spread:
  100 x 60 cm (40 x 24 in)
Blooming period:
  Summer
Soil type:
  Fertile, well-drained soil
Sun or Shade:
  Likes full sun
Hardiness:
  Minimum temp –18°C (0°F)

Physostegia virginiana • *Obedient Plant*

DESCRIPTION

A member of the mint family (Lamiaceae), Physostegia is a North American genus made up of two species of upright perennials. Physostegia is derived from the Greek *physo*, a bladder, and *stege*, a covering, referring to the way the calyx covers the fruit.

P. virginiana – known as obedient plant because the flowers stay in place when twisted – is a vigorous plant from eastern USA that spreads by rhizomes to form clumps of upright unbranched stems with narrow, toothed, lance-shaped, dark green leaves. Narrow conical flower spikes to 20 cm (8 in) long develop at the stem tips and bear downy, tubular, 5-lobed, purple-pink flowers to 30 mm (1¼ in) long, from summer to autumn. This is a hardy plant, easily grown in favourable conditions, but it can become invasive, however, provided the clumps are broken up occasionally this causes few problems. 'Variegata' has white-edged grey-green leaves. Propagate by division.

ABOVE: The common name for the species is 'Obedient Plant' because the flowers can be rotated or twisted to new positions and will remain this way and continue to grow.

Species, variety or cultivar:
  'Variegata'
Other common names:
  Obedient Plant
Height and spread:
  120 x 50 cm (48 x 20 in)
Blooming period:
  Summer to autumn
Soil type:
  Moist, well-drained soil
Sun or Shade:
  Prefers full sun to part-shade
Hardiness:
  Minimum temp –29°C (–20°F)

Phytolacca americana • *Poke*

DESCRIPTION

Found in temperate, warm-temperate and subtropical regions, Phytolacca comprises only 35 species of perennials, subshrubs and deciduous or evergreen shrubs and trees.

P. americana comes from North and Central America. The young stems are purple-red. During autumn, the large leaves turn purple-red and have pink tones. The tiny, cream, petal-less flowers are produced in drooping racemes and are followed by clusters of conspicuous berries that turn red and purple-black as they ripen. Winter is often the best time to prune, as it will not affect the flower and fruit production or autumn colour. Propagate from seed, rooted basal shoots or from cuttings during the growing season.

Species, variety or cultivar:
  –
Other common names:
  Poke, Pokeberry,
  Pokeweed
Height and spread:
  3.5 x 0.9 m (12 x 3 ft)
Blooming period:
  Summer
Soil type:
  Moist, moderately fertile,
  well-drained soil
Sun or Shade:
  Prefers full sun
Hardiness:
  Minimum temp –34°C
  (–30°F)

Pilosella aurantiaca

DESCRIPTION

A member of the daisy (Asteraceae) family, this genus is made up of 18 rhizomatous and hairy perennial herbs, which are native to temperate Eurasia and northwestern Africa.

P. auriantiaca is a perennial herb native to Europe. It forms rosettes of pale green, hairy, oval to elliptical leaves that can measure up to 20 cm (8 in) long. This species produces two to 25 umbrella-shaped flowerheads at the ends of tall hairy stalks. The orange to orange-red florets are borne in summer. Propagate from seed germinated in late winter or early spring; transplant in late spring. Can be invasive.

Species, variety or cultivar:
    –
Other common names:
    –
Height and spread:
    70 x 50 cm (27 x 20 in)
Blooming period:
    Summer
Soil type:
    Well-drained fertile soil
Sun or Shade:
    Likes full sun
Hardiness:
    Minimum temp –40°C (–40°F)

Platycodon grandiflorus • *Balloon Flower*

DESCRIPTION

There is only a single species in this genus in the bellflower (Campanulaceae) family. *P. grandiflorus* is a vigorous herbaceous perennial found in Japan and nearby parts of China, which forms a clump of broad, lance-shaped, toothed leaves. Opening from enlarged, balloon-like buds, the white, pink or blue flowers are cup- to bell-shaped with five broad lobes. Summer is the main flowering time.

There are a number of attractive cultivars and double-flowered and dwarf forms are common. The species may be raised from seed; cultivars are propagated by division. Initially slow to establish, this plant is very hardy and long-lived, though it does best in a temperate climate with distinct seasons. This plant and its many cultivars make ideal subjects for rock gardens, or can be used to add colour to herbaceous borders. Platycodon root, used in traditional Chinese medicine, is being studied for its mutagenic effects on tumors.

Species, variety or cultivar:
–

Other common names:
Balloon Flower, Chinese Bellflower

Height and spread:
70 x 60 cm (27 x 24 in)

Blooming period:
Summer

Soil type:
Moist, humus-rich, well-drained soil

Sun or Shade:
Enjoys full sun to part-shade

Hardiness:
Minimum temp –34°C (–30°F)

Polemonium caeruleum • *Charity*

DESCRIPTION

This genus of 25 erect or spreading, or
rhizomatous annual or sometimes short-lived
perennial herbs belongs to the phlox
(Polemoniaceae) family. A native of northern
and central Europe and northern Asia,
P. caeruleum is a hairy and glandular
perennial. Growing from a central base, the
pinnate leaves are up to 40 cm (16 in) long
with sword-shaped to oblong leaflets. From
late spring to summer, loose heads of flowers
are produced, with blue, occasionally white,
widely bell-shaped corollas. 'Brise d'Anjou', is
a stunning variegated form. Propagate by
division in autumn or early spring, or from
seed sown in autumn or winter.

Species, variety or cultivar:
 'Brise d'Anjou'
Other common names:
 Charity, Greek Valerian, Jacob's
 Ladder
Height and spread:
 90 x 50 cm (36 x 20 in)
Blooming period:
 Spring to summer
Soil type:
 Rich, well-drained, moist, loamy soil
Sun or Shade:
 Likes full sun
Hardiness:
 Minimum temp –40°C (–40°F)

Polygonatum cirrhifolium • *Solomon's Seal*

DESCRIPTION

Found in the temperate zones of the Northern Hemisphere, there are approximately 50 species in this genus, which is a member of the lily-of-the-valley (Convallariaceae) family. Spreading by underground rhizomes, most of these easy-to-grow herbaceous perennials are fully hardy.

A native of China, *P. cirrhifolium* forms whorls of long thin leaves that curl slightly at the tips. The narrow, tubular, creamy coloured flowers, with tips sometimes differently coloured, are borne in late spring to early summer, and are followed by red berries in autumn. Propagate from seeds or divide the rhizomes in spring or autumn. Cut the stems down to soil level in late autumn.

Species, variety or cultivar:
  –
Other common names:
  Solomon's Seal
Height and spread:
  2 x 0.6 m (7 x 2 ft)
Blooming period:
  Late spring to early summer
Soil type:
  Rich, moist, peaty soil
Sun or Shade:
  Prefers shade
Hardiness:
  Minimum temp –23°C
  (–10°F)

Potentilla fruticosa • *Cinquefoil*

DESCRIPTION

This large genus of some 500 species, mostly herbaceous perennials, belongs to the rose (Rosaceae) family. The shrubby species are exceptionally useful as small ornamentals, being very hardy, thriving in most soils, in sun and in partial shade.

Distributed widely through the Northern Hemisphere, *P. fruticosa* is a dense shrub. The small leaves are palmately arranged, and are divided into five to seven narrow leaflets. The striking yellow flowers, which resemble small single roses, are borne during summer and autumn. The many cultivars come in a range of colours, mostly yellow, orange, pink, red and cream.

Species, variety or cultivar:
'Primrose Beauty'
Other common names:
Cinquefoil, Potentilla, Shrubby Cinquefoil
Height and spread:
1.5 x 1.5 m (5 x 5 ft)
Blooming period:
Summer to autumn
Soil type:
Fertile, well-drained soil
Sun or Shade:
Enjoys full sun
Hardiness:
Minimum temp –40°C (–40°F)

One such example is 'Primrose Beauty' with rich cream flowers.

Cultivars with orange, red, or pink flowers tend to fade in very strong sunshine and should be given a position where they receive some shade in the hottest part of the day. Propagation is usually from seed in autumn or cuttings in summer.

Primula auricula • *Cowslip*

DESCRIPTION

Though widespread, this genus of perennials is primarily from the Northern Hemisphere, and gives its name to the family Primulaceae. The genus acquired its name from the Italian word for spring – primavera.

P. auricula is native to the mountains of southern Europe. This clump-forming plant has fleshy light green leaves that are usually toothed. Both the stems and leaves have a mealy coating. It bears heads of few to many flat, 12–25 mm (½–1 in) wide flowers, which in the wild are most often yellow or purple-red with yellow centres. The flowers of 'Lucy Locket' are buff yellow with a cream centre.

Species, variety or cultivar:
'Lucy Locket'
Other common names:
Cowslip, Polyanthus, Primrose
Height and spread:
20 x 40 cm (8 x 16 in)
Blooming period:
Spring
Soil type:
Moist, humus-rich, well-drained soil
Sun or Shade:
Prefers part-shade to full shade
Hardiness:
Minimum temp –40°C (–40°F)

Primula denticulata • *Drumstick Primula*

DESCRIPTION

Primula is a large genus of perennials, belonging to the self-named family Primulaceae. Most primulas form basal rosettes of heavily veined leaves from which the flower stems emerge, usually with a large terminal head or several well-shaped whorls of flowers, but sometimes with just a single bloom.

P. denticulata is a perennial from mountains of Afghanistan to Myanmar. It overwinters as a conical bud, in spring producing rounded heads of mauve to purple-red flowers, rarely white, with or before the new leaves. Both the flower stems and undersides of the toothed leaves are downy white. Propagate from seed or by dividing well-established clumps when dormant.

Species, variety or cultivar:
–

Other common names:
Drumstick Primula

Height and spread:
20 x 45 cm (12 x 18 in)

Blooming period:
Spring

Soil type:
Moist, humus-rich, well-drained soil

Sun or Shade:
Prefers full shade to part-shade

Hardiness:
Minimum temp –29°C (–20°F)

Prunella grandiflora • *Bigflower*

DESCRIPTION

Native to temperate Eurasia, North Africa and North America, this genus of seven semi-evergreen, spreading, sprawling, then climbing perennial herbs belongs to the mint (Lamiaceae) family.

P. grandiflora is a mat-forming herb from Europe. Well suited to rock gardens, it has woody, branching, slightly hairy stems covered with tiny, oval to sword-shaped leaves that have scalloped edges. Showy heads of densely whorled spikelets of four to six off-white, pale blue or purple flowers with an erect, hooded, 2-lipped, deep violet corolla with three lobes, are borne on stubby stalks surrounded by leaf-like bracts. 'Loveliness' has attractive pale lilac flowers.

Species, variety or cultivar:
'Loveliness'

Other common names:
Bigflower, Large Self-heal, Self-heal

Height and spread:
60 x 60 cm (24 x 24 in)

Blooming period:
Summer

Soil type:
Dry to moist, well-drained soil

Sun or Shade:
Likes full sun

Hardiness:
Minimum temp –34°C (–30°F)

Pterocephalus perennis

DESCRIPTION

This genus of around 25 species is a member of the teasel (Dipsacaceae) family. These compact, annual or perennial herbs and small shrubs are found from the Mediterranean to central and eastern Asia.

P. perennis (syns *P. bellidifolius*, *P. involucratus*, *P. parnassi*) is a semi-evergreen, cushion-forming, tufted perennial found growing in grassland and rocks in subalpine to alpine Greece and Albania. The greyish green leaves are oblong to oval, finely hairy and crinkled. Large, tight, rounded heads of tubular, purplish pink flowers, surrounded by narrow bracts, are borne in summer. The flowers are followed by feathery seed heads. This plant self-seeds readily.

Species, variety or cultivar:
–

Other common names:
–

Height and spread:
10 x 20 cm (4 x 8 in)

Blooming period:
Summer

Soil type:
Well-drained soil

Sun or Shade:
Enjoys full sun

Hardiness:
Minimum temp –34°C (–30°F)

Pulmonaria longifolia • *Lungwort*

DESCRIPTION

This genus of 14 Eurasian perennials in the borage (Boraginaceae) family is indispensable for woodland, perennial border and rock garden cultivation. While welcome, the first flowers are sparse, but the plants carry larger heads of small 5-petalled blooms as the flowering season progresses.

P. *longifolia* is a very hardy European species that forms a clump of narrow, often white-spotted, dark green leaves to 50 cm (20 in) long. Heads of tightly clustered mauve to purple-blue flowers occur in late winter to late spring. 'Bertram Anderson' has especially narrow, heavily white-spotted leaves and bright blue flowers. Propagate by division, or from basal cuttings or seed.

Species, variety or cultivar:
 'Bertram Anderson'
Other common names:
 Lungwort
Height and spread:
 40 x 120 cm (16 x 48 in)
Blooming period:
 Late winter to late spring
Soil type:
 Moist, humus-rich, well-drained soil
Sun or Shade:
 Can be grown in sun but do best in part- to full shade
Hardiness:
 Minimum temp −23°C (−10°F)

Pulmonaria saccharata • *Jerusalem Sage*

DESCRIPTION

Commonly known as lungwort, this genus contains 14 species, all hardy perennials from Eurasia. 'Wort' is a word often attached to plants with medicinal uses. These resilient plants do best in a temperate climate with distinct seasons.

From northern Italy, the flowers of *P. saccharata* appear after the foliage is well developed. The spring leaves are small, lance-shaped and spotted; the summer leaves are larger. The dainty, small, 5-petalled blooms of white, shades of mauve to purple or purple-red, appear in spring. The cultivar 'Leopard' has white-spotted leaves and red-pink flowers. Propagate from basal cuttings or seed, or by division.

Species, variety or cultivar:
  'Leopard'
Other common names:
  Jerusalem Sage
Height and spread:
  40 x 80 cm (16 x 32 in)
Blooming period:
  Spring
Soil type:
  Moist, humus-rich, well-drained soil
Sun or Shade:
  Does best in part- to full shade
Hardiness:
  Minimum temp –40°C (–40°F)

Pulsatilla vulgaris • *Pasque Flower*

DESCRIPTION

These 30-odd deciduous perennials in this genus, a member of the buttercup (Ranunculaceae) family, are native to Eurasia and North America. These relatives of the anemones race into growth in early spring. The meaning of the genus name, taken from the Latin pulso, 'to strike,' is obscure, possibly referring to the drooping buds turning upwards as they open.

Found from Britain through Europe to Ukraine, *P. vulgaris* is entirely covered in fine, silky, silvery hairs. Forming clumps, the feathery leaves are very finely divided. Many long stems of usually upward-facing, open bell-shaped, 5–8 cm (2–3 in) wide, mauve to purple flowers, are produced in spring. Carried singly, they have five to eight petals and a prominent boss of golden stamens. 'Papageno' (syn. *P. v. subsp. grandis* 'Papageno') is a mixed colour strain in many shades, including apricot and purple-black. Propagate by division when dormant, or raise from seed.

Species, variety, or cultivar:
'Papageno'
Other common names:
Pasque Flower
Height and spread:
38 x 40 cm (15 x 16 in)
Blooming period:
Spring
Soil type:
Gritty, humus-rich, well-drained, yet moist soil
Sun or Shade:
Enjoys full sun to part-shade
Hardiness:
Minimum temp –29°C (–20°F)

LEFT: The cultivar name of 'Papageno' was most likely borrowed from the brightly coloured bird-catcher character of the same name in Mozart's *The Magic Flute* opera. Pasque comes from Old French for Easter in reference to the spring bloom time. Vulgaris means common.

Ramonda myconi

DESCRIPTION

Evergreen, rosette-forming, alpine plants, the three species in this genus are found from the mountains of northeastern Spain to the Balkans.

R. myconi (syn. *R. pyrenaica*) is a charming rosette-forming perennial from northeastern Spain. It features rich green leaves that are crinkled, hairy and heavily veined. The clusters of violet-blue flowers, which are held well above the leaves in late spring and early summer, are 4- or 5-petalled, more or less flat-faced, to 25 mm (1 in) across, with yellow anthers. Propagation is quite difficult from seed. They are usually propagated by division or, better still, from leaf cuttings taken in late summer.

Species, variety or cultivar:
–
Other common names:
–
Height and spread:
12 x 20 cm (5 x 8 in)
Blooming period:
Late spring to early summer
Soil type:
Well-drained soil
Sun or Shade:
Likes part-shade
Hardiness:
Minimum temp –23°C (–10°F)

Ranunculus asiaticus • *Buttercup*

DESCRIPTION

This widespread group encompasses some 400 species of annuals, biennials and perennials, and is the type genus for its family, the Ranunculaceae. Many of the species are cultivated, others are admired in the wild, and some are despised as invasive weeds.

R. *asiaticus* is a rhizome-rooted southern Eurasian perennial with finely divided, ferny, basal leaves. Appearing in late spring to summer, the large, often double flowers, are held on hairy upright stems, and are mainly in yellow to red shades in the wild. The cultivated forms come in many colours, and are often sold as mixed colour strains. Propagate by division or from seed.

Species, variety or cultivar:
 –
Other common names:
  Buttercup
Height and spread:
  45 x 30 cm (18 x 12 in)
Blooming period:
  Late spring to summer
Soil type:
  Well-drained soil
Sun or Shade:
  Enjoys full sun to part-
  shade
Hardiness:
  Minimum temp –12°C
  (10°F)

Ranunculus lyallii • *Mount Cook Buttercup*

DESCRIPTION

Commonly known as buttercups, this large genus of around 400 species has a worldwide distribution. Ranunculus is a Latin word meaning 'little frog,' referring to the wet conditions in which most wild buttercups are found. Many species can be invasive, so take care to plant where they can be controlled.

A perennial from damp subalpine areas of New Zealand's South Island, *R. lyallii* has leathery, glossy dark green, kidney-shaped leaves that can reach up to 40 cm (16 in) wide. In late spring to early summer, the tall branching stems bear panicles of pure white flowers. Propagate by division or from seed.

Species, variety or cultivar:
–

Other common names:
Mount Cook Buttercup, Mount Cook Lily

Height and spread:
120 x 120 cm (48 x 48 in)

Blooming period:
Late spring to early summer

Soil type:
Well-drained soil

Sun or Shade:
Prefers part- to full shade

Hardiness:
Minimum temp −18°C (0°F)

Raoulia hookeri • *Mat Daisy*

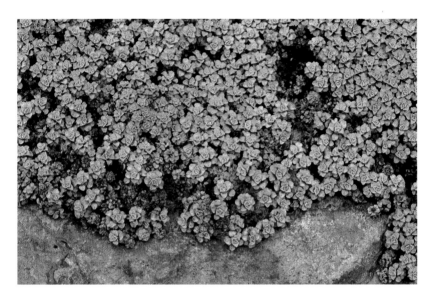

DESCRIPTION

Native to New Zealand, there are 20 to 30
species of tiny-leafed, mat- or cushion-forming,
evergreen perennials or subshrubs in this genus,
which belongs to the daisy (Asteraceae) family.
The largest cushion-forming species is commonly
known as vegetable sheep because from a
distance the plant looks like a sheep sitting down!

Found on New Zealand's South Island and
southern regions of North Island, growing from
sea level to 1,800 m (5,900 ft), *R. hookeri* is a
dense mat-forming plant with tiny silvery leaves.
It bears creamy white flowers in summer.
Propagate from seed or sections of the mat
(rooted stems).

Species, variety or cultivar:
–
Other common names:
Mat Daisy, Scabweed
Height and spread:
3 x 60 cm (1¼ x 24 in)
Blooming period:
Summer
Soil type:
Moist, well-drained soil
Sun or Shade:
Enjoys full sun to part-shade
Hardiness:
Minimum temp –18°C (0°F)

Rehmannia angulata • *Chinese Foxglove*

DESCRIPTION

Grown for their large exotic-looking flowers that enjoy a long flowering season, this genus contains around nine species of herbaceous perennials from the woods and hills of China. The genus is a member of the foxglove (Scrophulariaceae) family, and the plants usually feature magenta-pink flowers patterned with brown and yellow in the throat, and heavily serrated, hairy to sticky foliage. They usually prefer a spot that receives plenty of light but not the very hottest sun.

From central China, *R. angulata* is a herbaceous perennial with heavily serrated, stemless leaves that form a basal rosette. It bears magenta trumpet-flowers 6 cm (2½ in) long, in spring to early summer. It is very rarely grown in its true form; the name is often incorrectly used for *R. elata* in horticulture. The cultivar 'Beverley Bells' features mauve-pink flowers. Propagate from seed, or from stem cuttings early in the growth cycle, or more usually by division.

BELOW: *Rehmannia angulata* is a much underrated perennial for woodland borders. The foxglove-like, magenta blooms with intricate spots give the name of Chinese Foxglove. Grow in a sheltered site, in fertile, well-drained soil.

Species, variety or cultivar:
  'Beverley Bells'
Other common names:
  Chinese Foxglove
Height and spread:
  30 x 40 cm (12 x 16 in)
Blooming period:
  Spring to early summer
Soil type:
  Moisture-retentive, but not wet,
  humus-rich soil
Sun or Shade:
  Prefers part-shade
Hardiness:
  Minimum temp –12°C (10°F)

Rhodohypoxis baurii • *Red Star*

DESCRIPTION

This southern African genus of about six low-growing, clump-forming, free-flowering, cormous perennials belongs to the star-flower (Hypoxidaceae) family. Coming from the damp-summer climates of southern Africa, they rarely thrive in wet-winter dry-summer climates without some assistance. In favourable conditions, these plants enjoy a long flowering period.

R. baurii is a perennial from South Africa. The dull grey-green, lance-shaped leaves are grass-like, tuft-forming and very hairy. Held on short stems, the upturned 6-petalled starry flowers, are almost flat. They come in shades of white through pink and red, and are produced throughout summer. 'Tetra Red' has large dark pink-red flowers.

Species, variety or cultivar:
 'Tetra Red'
Other common names:
 Red Star, Rosy Posy
Height and spread:
 10 x 10 cm (4 x 4 in)
Blooming period:
 Summer
Soil type:
 Lime-free soil
Sun or Shade:
 Enjoys full sun
Hardiness:
 Minimum temp −12°C (10°F)

Rodgersia pinnata

DESCRIPTION

Found among the woodlands and streamsides of temperate Asia, the six large perennials in this genus are members of the saxifrage (Saxifragaceae) family. Although they have a preference for damp conditions, they are not happy in stagnant boggy conditions, and usually do better alongside moving water.

R. pinnata is a perennial from southwestern China. The leaves are partly pinnate, with five to nine dark green, deeply veined leaflets, to 20 cm (8 in) long. Held on long stems above the foliage, the panicles of deep pink to red, rarely white flowers appear in summer. 'Rosea' features attractive deep pink flowers.

Species, variety or cultivar:
  'Rosea'
Other common names:
  –
Height and spread:
  1.2 x 2 m (4 x 7 ft)
Blooming period:
  Summer
Soil type:
  Cool, moist, humus-rich soil
Sun or Shade:
  Prefers full sun or partial shade
Hardiness:
  Minimum temp –23°C (–10°F)

Romneya coulteri • *California Tree Poppy*

DESCRIPTION

Native to western North America and Mexico, this genus of just two species belongs to the poppy (Papaveraceae) family. They share similar deeply cut, blue-green foliage and large, 6-petalled, white, poppy-like flowers that are pleasantly scented. While they are initially sometimes difficult to establish, allow plenty of space when planting, as once they are settled the underground stems spread quickly. Once established, they resent being transplanted. They do well in a warm sunny position, and can become invasive in some situations.

With persistent stems and finely cut silvery grey leaves that may be toothed or smooth edged, *R. coulteri* is a small to medium-sized

Species, variety or cultivar:
–
Other common names:
California Tree Poppy, Matalija Poppy
Height and spread:
2.4 x 2 m (8 x 7 ft)
Blooming period:
Late summer to mid-autumn
Soil type:
Fertile, well-drained soil
Sun or Shade:
Likes full sun
Hardiness:
Minimum temp −18°C (0°F)

perennial native to southern California, USA. The smooth, slightly conical, solitary buds open to reveal large fragrant flowers, up to 15 cm (6 in) across, with crumpled, crape-like, white petals arranged around a bold central boss of golden yellow stamens. Propagation is from seed or cuttings.

LEFT: The common name is pronounced *ma-tilli-ha*. This is a direct reference from the Indian name for Matalija Canyon in Ventura county, California.

Rudbeckia fulgida • *Black-Eyed Susan*

DESCRIPTION

The 15 species of perennials in this genus are
hardy reliable plants belonging to the daisy
(Asteraceae) family. These easily grown plants
are popular with gardeners for their late-
season flowering display.

R. *fulgida* is a perennial from southeastern
USA. The lance-shaped leaves can be bristly,
and are often over 10 cm (4 in) long.
Throughout summer and autumn, it produces
flowerheads to nearly 8 cm (3 in) wide, with
yellow to orange ray florets and dark purple-
brown disc florets. R. *f. var. sullivantii* grows
to 90 cm (36 in) tall, with larger flowerheads
and pointed oval, often downy leaves.

Species, variety or cultivar:
  var. sullivantii
Other common names:
  Black-eyed Susan, Orange
  Coneflower
Height and spread:
  100 x 120 cm (40 x 48 in)
Blooming period:
  Summer to autumn
Soil type:
  Moist, well-drained soil
Sun or Shade:
  Enjoys full sun to part-shade
Hardiness:
  Minimum temp −34°C (−30°F)

Ruschia dichroa • *Ice Plant*

DESCRIPTION

Comprising about 400 species of perennials and succulent shrubs, this large genus is native to the drier parts of southern Africa, and belongs to the iceplant (Aizoaceae) family. The attractive, purple, pink, sometimes white, daisy flowers may be solitary or in branched flowerheads.

R. dichroa is a succulent perennial from coastal western South Africa, which features dark reddish brown internodes and paired leaves up to 6 cm (2½ in) long. In summer, purple, white or pink daisies, 4 cm (1¾ in) across, are produced. Propagate from stem cuttings, which can be rooted at almost any time of year.

Species, variety or cultivar:
–
Other common names:
Ice Plant
Height and spread:
30 x 40 cm (12 x 16 in)
Blooming period:
Summer
Soil type:
Poor, well-drained soil
Sun or Shade:
Likes full sun
Hardiness:
Minimum temp –1°C (30°F)

Sagina subulata • *Golden Pearlwort*

DESCRIPTION

The approximately 20 species of ground covering, mat-forming plants in this Northern Hemisphere genus grow on rocky outcrops. Many are garden weeds and are difficult to eradicate because of their highly developed reproduction system. Fine linear leaves are

arranged in pairs and they quickly form dense mats that cover the soil and rocky areas. Pearlworts do not like prolonged periods of hot dry weather, preferring cool temperatures and cool free-draining soils in full sun or part-shade. *S. subulata* is a mat-forming perennial with soft foliage from central Europe, which forms dense mounds and bears solitary white flowers in summer.

Species, variety or cultivar:
–

Other common names:
Golden Pearlwort

Height and spread:
2.5 x 30 cm (1 x 12 in)

Blooming period:
Summer

Soil type:
Cool, free-draining soil

Sun or Shade:
Likes full sun or part-shade

Hardiness:
Minimum temp –34°C (–30°F)

Saintpaulia • *African Violet*

DESCRIPTION

The botanically inclined German soldier Walter von Saint Paul discovered this tropical East Africa genus of 20 perennials. They are soft-stemmed, rosette-forming plants with finely hairy, rounded leaves that have toothed edges and long petioles.

Most of the widely grown African violets are cultivars of *S. ionantha*, though some are true hybrids between *S. ionantha* and other species, such as *S. shumensis*. Clusters of velvety 5-petalled flowers appear at the centre of the rosettes throughout the year, ranging from mainly pink to purple tones but also including white, near-red shades and yellow. 'Hisako' is a deep purple-blue cultivar with fine white edges.

Species, variety or cultivar:
  hybrid cultivar, 'Hisako'
Other common names:
  African Violet
Height and spread:
  20 x 30 cm (8 x 12 in)
Blooming period:
  Throughout the year
Soil type:
  Fertile, moist, humus-rich soil
Sun or Shade:
  Bright but not sunny conditions
Hardiness:
  Minimum temp 4°C (40°F)

Salvia argentea • *Silver Sage*

DESCRIPTION

This genus, the largest in the mint (Lamiaceae) family, contains about 900 species of annuals, perennials and softwooded evergreen shrubs. They grow in a wide range of habitats, from coastal to alpine, but over half the species are native to the Americas.

Most are best grown in full sun and all require a well-drained situation. Prune in spring to remove straggly, bare and frost-damaged stems.

S. argentea is a perennial, native to southern Europe, with large woolly leaves of a silvery appearance, to 100 cm (40 in) long, on a basal rosette of foliage. Tall candelabra-like stems of white flowers are produced in the second year.

Species, variety or cultivar:
–
Other common names:
  Silver Sage
Height and spread:
  60 x 100 cm (24 x 40 in)
Blooming period:
  Summer
Soil type:
  Well-drained soil
Sun or Shade:
  Does best in full sun
Hardiness:
  Minimum temp –12°C (10°F)

Salvia farinacea • *Mealy Sage*

DESCRIPTION

The leaves of this genus are carried on squared hairy stems, and are aromatic when crushed. The flowers are tubular with the petals split into two lips, which may be straight or flaring, and the colour range extends through shades of blue to purple, and pink to red, as well as white and some yellows.

S. farinacea is from Texas and New Mexico, and from summer to autumn flowers are borne at the ends of the stems, in shades of blue, purple or white, and dusted in a flour-like substance. The cultivar 'Victoria Blue' has a shorter habit and larger flowers, which are a deep blue.

Species, variety or cultivar:
  'Victoria Blue'
Other common names:
  Mealy Sage
Height and spread:
  120 x 60 cm (48 x 24 in)
Blooming period:
  Summer to autumn
Soil type:
  Well-drained soil
Sun or Shade:
  Prefers full sun
Hardiness:
  Minimum temp –7°C (20°F)

Sandersonia aurantiaca • *Chinese Lantern Lily*

DESCRIPTION

A deciduous, scrambling to climbing, tuberous perennial, this species is the sole member of the genus named for John Sanderson (1820–91), honorary secretary to the Horticultural Society of Natal. A member of the autumn-crocus (Colchiaceae) family, and now rare in its native South African habitat, this decorative plant is widely grown in gardens and for the cut-flower trade. The leaves are soft-green, and alternate along the stems, and the tip often becomes a tendril by which it scrambles. Flowers are a glowing golden orange, lantern-shaped and pendent, on downturned stalks, and are borne in summer.

Species, variety or cultivar:
  –
Other common names:
  Chinese Lantern Lily,
  Christmas Bells
Height and spread:
  100 x 20 cm (40 x 8 in)
Blooming period:
  Summer
Soil type:
  Poor soils are tolerated,
  and may even be
  preferable
Sun or Shade:
  Prefers full sun
Hardiness:
  Minimum temp –7°C (20°F)

Sanguinaria canadensis • *Bloodroot*

DESCRIPTION

S. canadensis is the single species in this genus from the poppy (Papaveraceae) family. A perennial woodland plant from eastern North America, it has large green-grey leaves with deep indentations. Small white or pinkish starry flowers, one per stalk, appear in spring, unfurling to reveal their rounded scalloped shape. This plant is an ephemeral and will die down by mid-summer – so mark its location. It will eventually spread to make a good woodland ground cover. The plant contains alkaloids and has been used medicinally as an emetic. 'Multiplex' is an attractive cultivar with showy double white flowers.

Species, variety or cultivar:
  'Multiplex'
Other common names:
  Bloodroot, Red Puccoon
Height and spread:
  20 x 10 cm (8 x 4 in)
Blooming period:
  Spring
Soil type:
  Rich, moist soil
Sun or Shade:
  Prefers half-sun or shade
Hardiness:
  Minimum temp –46°C (–50°F)

Saponaria ocymoides • *Rock Soapwort*

DESCRIPTION

This genus in the pink (Caryophyllaceae) family contains some 20 species of temperate Eurasian annuals and perennials that contain saponin, a glycoside that forms a soapy colloidal solution when mixed with water. The roots in particular were once used as soap, and the extract is present in detergents and foaming agents.

S. ocymoides is a mound-forming alpine perennial found from Spain to the Balkans, with small, downy, blue-green linear to spatula-shaped leaves, sometimes toothed. Clusters of 12 mm (½ in) wide, starry, 5-petalled, deep pink flowers, less commonly red or white, smother the plant in summer.

Species, variety or cultivar:
–
Other common names:
Rock Soapwort
Height and spread:
30 x 50 cm (12 x 20 in)
Blooming period:
Summer
Soil type:
Gritty, moist, humus-rich, free-draining soil
Sun or Shade:
Likes full sun
Hardiness:
Minimum temp –40°C (–40°F)

Saponaria officinalis • *Soapwort*

DESCRIPTION

Although the roots of the roughly 20 species in this genus were once used as soap, and the extract is still present in detergents and foaming agents, these are pretty little plants that are well worth growing for their beauty alone. They are mainly low growing and range from tufted mounds to quite wide-spreading ground covers.

S. officinalis is a perennial found over much of Europe, and is a large billowing mound of wiry stems, green to grey-green, with pointed oval leaves. Heads of five or more flowers, usually bright pink, are borne in late summer to autumn. 'Rosea Plena' has tall pink double flowers.

Species, variety or cultivar:
  'Rosea Plena'
Other common names:
  Bouncing Bet, Soapwort
Height and spread:
  60 x 100 cm (24 x 40 in)
Blooming period:
  Autumn
Soil type:
  Gritty, moist, humus-rich, free-draining soil
Sun or Shade:
  Prefers full sun
Hardiness:
  Minimum temp –34°C (–30°F)

Sarracenia flava • *Yellow Trumpet*

DESCRIPTION

The eight species of Sarracenia are beautiful carnivorous American pitcher-plants in the Sarraceniaceae family. They hybridize easily both in the wild and in cultivation, and are found in swamps, wetlands and pine forest edges, mainly in southeastern USA. They are perennial, grow from a rhizome and the leaves or pitchers form a basal rosette. Most have long tubular pitchers and stunning, nodding, scented flowers that grow singly on tall leafless stalks. Inside, downward-pointing hairs prevent prey – usually small insects – escaping from a well of digestive liquid. Grow in full sun in peat moss or a mix of peat and sand. Water by tray and keep the water level constant.

S. *flava* is a varied pitcher plant found along USA's Atlantic coastal plain. They are tall pitchers, widening towards the mouth, with large green lids, and the flowers, yellow to greenish yellow, appear in spring. 'Red Veined' is veined red, and red around the throat.

LEFT: The Yellow Pitcher Plant is a carnivorous plant that prefers wasps, bees and all types of flies. It needs high moisture therefore and is usually found among mosses. The large erect leaves possess desirable ornamental value. Its flowers are yellow rising in the spring, born on stalks that clear the foliage.

Species, variety or cultivar:
  'Red Veined'
Other common names:
  Yellow Trumpet
Height and spread:
  75 x 30 cm (30 x 12 in)
Blooming period:
  Spring
Soil type:
  Peat moss or a mix of peat and sand
Sun or Shade:
  Needs full sun
Hardiness:
  Minimum temp –18°C (0°F)

Saxifraga globulifera

DESCRIPTION

The genus Saxifraga from the Saxifragaceae family is very extensive, comprising a wide range of perennial, annual or biennial ground-hugging plants, many of which are alpines. They are found throughout much of the temperate and subarctic zones of the Northern Hemisphere, with outposts in places such as Ethiopia, Mexico and the Arctic.

S. globulifera is a mounding perennial found on both sides of the Straits of Gibraltar with short, leafy, erect stems, and rosettes of small 5-lobed leaves. White flowers are to 10 mm (½ in) wide, in heads on stems to 15 cm (6 in) long, and are borne in autumn to spring.

Species, variety or cultivar:
–
Other common names:
–
Height and spread:
20 x 30 cm (8 x 12 in)
Blooming period:
Autumn to spring
Soil type:
Free-draining, relatively fertile soil
Sun or Shade:
Either full sun or part-shade
Hardiness:
Minimum temp –18°C (0°F)

Saxifraga oppositifolia • *Purple Mountain Saxifrage*

DESCRIPTION

There are some 480 known species of Saxifraga, many of which are well worth growing, and numerous garden hybrids. A major attraction for many gardeners is that the plants are not only diverse in themselves but also come from a variety of habitats such as exposed mountains and moist woodlands.

S. oppositifolia is a clumping and dense mat-forming perennial from arctic mountains of Europe, western Asia and North America, and has rosettes of stiff, elliptical, dark green leaves. Single, almost stemless, dark red to purple flowers, appear in summer. Being shallow-rooted plants, they require free-draining relatively fertile soil in either sun or part-shade.

Species, variety or cultivar:
–

Other common names:
Purple Mountain Saxifrage

Height and spread:
2.5 x 20 cm (1 x 8 in)

Blooming period:
Summer

Soil type:
Free-draining, relatively fertile soil

Sun or Shade:
Likes both full sun and part-shade

Hardiness:
Minimum temp –51°C (–60°F)

Scabiosa caucasica • *Scabious*

DESCRIPTION

An unpleasant sounding name, Scabiosa is derived from scabies, a Latin word for scurf or mange, which was said to be relieved by rubbing with the leaves of these plants. A member of the teasel (Dipsacaceae) family, the genus comprises around 80 species of annuals and perennials found from Europe and North Africa to Japan.

S. *caucasica* is a perennial from the Caucasus, Russia with grey-green to blue-green leaves, lance-shaped, large, smooth-edged basal foliage, and upper leaves that are lobed, almost to midrib. Powder blue flowers in heads to 8 cm (3 in) wide, appear in summer to autumn. 'Clive Greaves' has delicate pale lavender blue flowers.

Species, variety or cultivar:
  'Clive Greaves'
Other common names:
  Scabious
Height and spread:
  90 x 45 cm (36 x 18 in)
Blooming period:
  Summer to autumn
Soil type:
  Fertile, moist, free-draining, slightly alkaline soil
Sun or Shade:
  Likes full or part-sun
Hardiness:
  Minimum temp–34°C (–30°F)

Scabiosa minoana • *Scabious*

DESCRIPTION

Most species in this genus form a spreading basal clump of light green to grey-green, rounded to lance-shaped leaves with deeply incised notches or lobes. A few species have an erect or branching habit. The flowers are individually tiny but occur in rounded to flattened composite heads on stems held clear of the foliage. White and pale yellow to soft pink or powder blue and mauve are the usual colours.

S. *minoana* is an evergreen shrub from southern Europe and the eastern Mediterranean, including Crete. It has rounded silver-haired leaves and small heads of lavender flowers, which are borne in summer.

Species, variety or cultivar:
–

Other common names:
Scabious

Height and spread:
60 x 50 cm (24 x 20 in)

Blooming period:
Summer

Soil type:
Fertile, moist, free-draining, slightly alkaline soil

Sun or Shade:
Enjoys full or part-sun

Hardiness:
Minimum temp –18°C (0°F)

Schizostylis coccinea • *Kaffir Lily*

DESCRIPTION

Native to the damp meadows of southern Africa, this genus consists of a single highly variable species *S. coccinea*, and belongs to the iris (Iridaceae) family. Almost evergreen, these plants require some moisture throughout the year. They are valued for their bright flowers, which are borne in autumn, sometimes surviving into the winter months. Although the plants can be untidy, they can be container-grown and make good cut flowers. The leaves are mid-green and grassy, with distinct midribs, and the cup-shaped flowers are held on spikes similar to Gladiolus. The petals are variably shaped, narrow and pointed or wide and rounded, from red to pink or white.

Species, variety or cultivar:
–
Other common names:
Kaffir Lily
Height and spread:
60 x 60 cm (24 x 24 in)
Blooming period:
Autumn
Soil type:
A permanently moist peaty loam
Sun or Shade:
Likes a sunny place
Hardiness:
Minimum temp –23°C (–10°F)

Scutellaria alpina • *Helmet Flower*

DESCRIPTION

This genus of about 300 species of annuals and perennials belongs to the mint (Lamiaceae) family. They are found mostly in temperate Northern Hemisphere regions, growing in scrub, open woodland and grassland. The roots are often rhizomatous and plants are erect or sprawling, ranging from 15 cm (6 in) to 1.2 m (4 ft) high.

S. *alpina* is a sprawling perennial found in mountains from southern Europe to Siberia. Often rooting at nodes, and with mats of small oval leaves, it has small flowers in crowded racemes, purple, often with yellow on lower lip, in late spring to early summer.

Species, variety or cultivar:
–
Other common names:
Helmet Flower, Skullcap
Height and spread:
25 x 45 cm (10 x 18 in)
Blooming period:
Summer
Soil type:
Any reasonable soil
Sun or Shade:
Likes full sun
Hardiness:
Minimum temp –29°C (–20°F)

Scutellaria orientalis • *Helmet Flower*

DESCRIPTION

The leaves of this genus are opposite and entire, sometimes pinnate or toothed. The 2-lipped tubular flowers emerge from hooded calyces which give the genus its common names. The blue, white, or yellow flowers are borne in summer, singly, in pairs, or on the ends of spikes. A number of species are grown ornamentally and some are used in herbal medicine for their anti-spasmodic properties.

S. orientalis is a subshrub forming a low mound, native to southeastern Europe, with small oval leaves, dark green above and woolly grey beneath. Dense racemes of lemon yellow flowers, sometimes tinged or spotted red, cover the plant in summer.

Species, variety or cultivar:
–

Other common names:
Helmet Flower, Skullcap

Height and spread:
45 x 25 cm (18 x 10 in)

Blooming period:
Summer

Soil type:
Any reasonable soil

Sun or Shade:
Prefers full sun

Hardiness:
Minimum temp –18°C (0°F)

Sedum spathulifolium • *Stonecrop*

DESCRIPTION

There are over 300 species in this Northern Hemisphere genus, differing greatly in form and foliage, but all with a low-spreading habit, as the name, from the Latin *sedo* (to sit) suggests. Most are also characterized by yellow 5-petalled flowers and appreciate water at flowering time but are otherwise drought tolerant.

S. spathulifolium is a clump-forming perennial from western North America that spreads by long runners. The fleshy leaves are spatula-shaped and mainly clustered in rosettes at the stem tips. Tiny bright yellow flowers, in crowded heads, appear in late spring to early summer. 'Purpureum' also has yellow flowers, but its foliage is tinged purple-red.

Species, variety or cultivar:
'Purpureum'

Other common names:
Stonecrop

Height and spread:
15 x 60 cm (6 x 24 in)

Blooming period:
Summer

Soil type:
Gritty, well-drained soil

Sun or Shade:
Enjoys full sun

Hardiness:
Minimum temp −18°C (0°F)

Sedum spurium • *Stonecrop*

DESCRIPTION

Sedum is a very diverse group of succulents from the stonecrop (Crassulaceae) family with many hybrids. Of Northern Hemisphere origins, with over 300 species, they vary enormously in foliage and form. Some are shrubby, with flattened, oval, grey-green leaves, others trail and have succulent jellybean-like leaves, and some form very compact mats. Most produce small heads of tiny, bright yellow, 5-petalled flowers in summer and autumn. The name is derived from the Latin *sedo* (to sit), referring to the low-spreading habit. Some species have been used medicinally and as salad vegetables.

 S. spurium is an evergreen mat-forming perennial from the Caucasus to northern Iran, with spreading branches and opposite pairs of rounded, fleshy, toothed leaves that are red-tinted in the sun. Heads of small purple-red flowers, rarely white or pink, on erect stems, are borne in summer. 'Dragon's Blood' has reddish pink flowers and gold to maroon leaves.

BELOW: *Sedum spurium* 'Dragon's Blood' makes a colourful ground cover for hot, dry sunny areas. Star-shaped flowers of wine red form a carpet of colour from late June until August. The rich green foliage becomes bronze in autumn. Semi-evergreen, they retain their foliage almost all year. Excellent for banks, slopes, borders or edgings.

Species, variety or cultivar:
 'Dragon's Blood'
Other common names:
 Stonecrop
Height and spread:
 15 x 50 cm (6 x 20 in)
Blooming period:
 Summer
Soil type:
 Gritty, well-drained soil
Sun or Shade:
 Likes full sun
Hardiness:
 Minimum temp −18°C (0°F)

Sempervivum calcareum • *Hens and Chickens*

DESCRIPTION

The roughly 40 species in this genus bear white, yellow, red or purplish flowers that are held in a cluster on stout, fleshy stems in summer. These plants are excellent for rock gardens and pots, and they require sandy, well-drained soil and dry conditions. Smaller species prefer to nest tightly in narrow crevices while the larger species need a more humus-rich soil.

S. *calcareum* is native to the Pyrenees, and grown for its attractive rosettes of grey-green leaves with brown tips. There are a number of cultivars, such as 'Mrs Giuseppi', which has grey-green rosettes and red-tipped leaves that darken in winter.

Species, variety or cultivar:
  'Mrs Giuseppi'
Other common names:
  Hens and Chickens, Houseleek
Height and spread:
  18 x 50 mm (0.75 x 2 in)
Blooming period:
  Summer
Soil type:
  Sandy, well-drained soil
Sun or Shade:
  Needs full sun
Hardiness:
  Minimum temp –23°C (–10°F)

Sempervivum • *Hens and Chickens*

DESCRIPTION

This genus, containing about 40 species of perennials, comes from the mountains of central and southern Europe through to Turkey and Iran, where it grows in rocks and crevices. Thick, fleshy leaves may be dull or glossy, and sometimes covered in a soft down of hairs. They form a flat, crowded rosette and spread by offsets, in time becoming a dense, tight mat.

Sempervivums hybridize freely and garden forms come in all manner of sizes and styles. Most are grown for their foliage, but a few have showy flowers too, such as 'Raspberry Ice', which has tight symmetrical red-tinted rosettes, fringed with white hairs, as well as attractive pink blooms.

Species, variety or cultivar:
  hybrid cultivar, 'Raspberry Ice'
Other common names:
  Hens and Chickens, Houseleek
Height and spread:
  20 x 40 cm (8 x 16 in)
Blooming period:
  Summer
Soil type:
  Sandy, well-drained soil
Sun or Shade:
  Prefers full sun
Hardiness:
  Minimum temp −23°C (−10°F)

Senecio cineraria • *Dusty Miller*

DESCRIPTION

There are 1,250 species in this cosmopolitan genus of trees, shrubs, lianas, annuals, biennials and perennials within the daisy (Asteraceae) family, one of the largest genera of flowering plants. Appearing with or without florets, the flowers are usually yellow but can be purple, white, red or blue. Many senecios are toxic to livestock.

S. *cineraria* is a mounding subshrub from southern Europe, which is naturalized in southern England. The intensely silver-white leaves are deeply dissected and lobed, and small heads of yellow daisy flowers are borne in summer. 'Silver Dust' has broad, deeply cut, pewter leaves.

Species, variety or cultivar:
'Silver Dust'

Other common names:
Dusty Miller, Sea Ragwort

Height and spread:
50 x 40 cm (20 x 16 in)

Blooming period:
Summer

Soil type:
Moderately fertile, well-drained soil

Sun or Shade:
Enjoys full sun

Hardiness:
Minimum temp –18°C (0°F)

Sidalcea malviflora • *Checkerbloom*

DESCRIPTION

Native to western North America, this genus of roughly 22 species is found growing on lime-free, sandy grasslands along streams, and in damp mountain meadows. An ideal and popular plant for perennial borders, there are a number of improved varieties available bred for better colour and length of flowering. Remove spent flower spikes for continuous blooming throughout summer.

  S. malviflora is a perennial found from Oregon, USA to Baja California, Mexico. It forms a clump of erect stems, with 7- to 9-lobed shallowly toothed leaves. Racemes of many pink to lavender flowers are borne from spring to autumn.

Species, variety or cultivar:
  –
Other common names:
  Checkerbloom
Height and spread:
  100 x 75 cm (40 x 30 in)
Blooming period:
  Spring to autumn
Soil type:
  Humus-rich, free-draining soil
Sun or Shade:
  Likes full sun or part-shade
Hardiness:
  Minimum temp –23°C (–10°F)

Sidalcea • *Prairie Mallow*

DESCRIPTION

This genus of about 22 annual and perennial species in the mallow (Malvaceae) family is native to western North America, where these plants grow on lime-free, sandy grasslands along streams, and in damp mountain meadows. Resembling a small hollyhock, to which they are related, they have glossy, round, palmately lobed basal leaves and stiffly upright flower spikes bearing stalkless or short-stemmed, white, pink or purple open, cup-shaped flowers at the ends. Popular and charming plants for perennial borders, there are many improved varieties bred for colour and length of flowering. They are free-flowering throughout summer if spent flower spikes are removed. They require a humus-rich, free-draining soil in the sun and may be propagated by division and from seed.

The hybrid cultivars, mostly with *S. malviflora* in their parentage, are compact heavy-blooming plants that usually hold their flowers well above foliage. 'Elsie Hugh' has triangular, ruffled leaves and dainty, shell pink, fringed flowers.

Species, variety or cultivar:
  hybrid cultivar, 'Elsie Hugh'
Other common names:
  Checkerbloom, Miniature
  Hollyhocks, Prairie Mallow,
Height and spread:
  0.7 x 0.6 m (2½ x 2 ft)
Blooming period:
  Summer
Soil type:
  Moist, humus-rich, well-drained
  soil
Sun or Shade:
  Likes full sun
Hardiness:
  Minimum temp –23°C (–10°F)

Sisyrinchium

DESCRIPTION

This genus has about 90 species of annuals and perennials from the iris (Iridaceae) family that are native to North and South America, but which have also been known to naturalize in other temperate countries. They produce clumps of stiff, upright, linear or sword-shaped leaves, which arch out into a fan shape. During the spring and summer months, clusters of trumpet-shaped flowers appear on spikes that hold the flowers just above the top of the foliage.

The hybrid cultivar 'Californian Skies' has dark green lance-shaped foliage that supports sturdy flower stems. Mid-blue flowers appear from summer to late autumn.

Species, variety or cultivar:
  hybrid cultivar, 'Californian Skies'
Other common names:
  –
Height and spread:
  30 x 20 cm (12 x 8 in)
Blooming period:
  Summer to autumn
Soil type:
  Moderately fertile, well-drained soil
Sun or Shade:
  Prefers full sun
Hardiness:
  Minimum temp –12°C (10°F)

Smilacina racemosa • *False Solomon's Seal*

DESCRIPTION

There are 25 species of rhizomatous perennials in this genus, which belongs to the lily-of-the-valley (Convallariaceae) family. They are native to Northern and Central America and Asia where they grow in shady and damp woodland areas. They have alternately arranged lance-shaped leaves on unbranched upright to arching stems to 0.9 m (3 ft) tall.

S. racemosa is native to USA and northern Mexico and has arching, downy, cane-like stems and several paired, pointed oval leaves to 15 cm (6 in) long. Tiny creamy white flowers in panicles to 15 cm (6 in) long, are borne in summer, followed by red-tinted green berries.

Species, variety or cultivar:
–
Other common names:
False Solomon's Seal, False Spikenard, Solomon's Zigzag
Height and spread:
90 x 120 cm (36 x 48 in)
Blooming period:
Summer
Soil type:
Deep fertile soil, moisture-retentive and neutral to slightly acid
Sun or Shade:
Likes part- to full shade
Hardiness:
Minimum temp –34°C (–30°F)

Soldanella alpina • *Alpine Snowbell*

DESCRIPTION

This genus, which belongs to the primrose (Primulaceae) family, contains ten species of tiny alpine perennials native to the European Alps, Carpathians and Balkans. They grow naturally in short damp turf and rocky places in the mountains and the flowering stems often penetrate snow cover in early spring.

S. alpina is a perennial from the Pyrenees and Alps, Europe, which has dark green, leathery, kidney-shaped to round leaves. Flowering stems to 15 cm (6 in) high, with two to four fringed violet flowers, bell-shaped with crimson markings inside, appear in spring to early summer. Plant in an open cool position with protection from hot midday sun.

Species, variety or cultivar:
–

Other common names:
Alpine Snowbell

Height and spread:
15 x 20 cm (6 x 8 in)

Blooming period:
Spring

Soil type:
Well-drained rich soil, neutral to slightly acid

Sun or Shade:
Enjoys full sun

Hardiness:
Minimum temp −29°C (−20°F)

Solidago canadensis • *Goldenrod*

DESCRIPTION

The roughly 100 species of perennials in this primarily North American genus form clumps of upright, sometimes branching stems, the upper half of which develops panicles of tiny golden yellow flowers. Often, by the time flowering starts in late summer, many of the lower leaves have withered somewhat. This late-flowering habit was used by Native Americans as a kind of floral calendar, as a guide to when the corn would be ripe.

S. canadensis is an erect species widespread in North America. Narrow lance-shaped leaves to 10 cm (4 in) long, have serrated edges, and short panicles of golden yellow flowers bloom in late summer to autumn.

Species, variety or cultivar:
–
Other common names:
  Goldenrod
Height and spread:
  150 x 100 cm (60 x 40 in)
Blooming period:
  Late summer to autumn
Soil type:
  Fertile, moist, well-drained soil
Sun or Shade:
  Likes full or part-sun
Hardiness:
  Minimum temp −12°C (10°F)

Stachys byzantina • *Lamb's Ears*

DESCRIPTION

About 300 species are in this genus, and in the wild these plants can be found in a range of situations, from dry mountain areas through to scrub areas, wastelands, meadows and streamsides, particularly in northern temperate zones. The foliage is often aromatic, lending itself to many uses in the ornamental garden.

S. byzantina is a ground-hugging perennial from the Caucasus to Iran with oblong to

elliptical grey-green leaves, covered in silvery white down and soft to the touch. Upright stems of pink to purple flowers are borne in late spring to early summer. 'Cotton Boll' (syn. *S. lanata*, *S. olympica*), has longer leaves and modified cottonball-like flowers.

Species, variety or cultivar:
  'Cotton Boll'
Other common names:
  Lamb's Ears, Woolly Betony
Height and spread:
  45 x 60 cm (18 x 24 in)
Blooming period:
  Summer
Soil type:
  Well-drained open soil
Sun or Shade:
  Prefers full sun
Hardiness:
  Minimum temp −34°C (−30°F)

Stachys macrantha • *Big Betony*

DESCRIPTION

There are around 300 species in this mint (Lamiaceae) family genus, and they range from stoloniferous and rhizomatous perennials through to a few evergreen shrubs. Flowers are tubular, sometimes hooded, and vary from red, pink and purple through to white and yellow.

S. macrantha is an upright, hairy perennial from northeastern Turkey and northwestern Iran with rosettes of wide, ovate, crinkly, veined, dark green leaves to 8 cm (3 in) long. Spikes of hooded dark cerise-purple flowers, 3 cm (1¾ in) wide, on erect stems, appear in summer, and 'Superba' (syn. *S. grandiflora*), is a cultivar with bright cerise-purple flowers.

Species, variety or cultivar:
  'Superba'
Other common names:
  Big Betony
Height and spread:
  60 x 45 cm (24 x 18 in)
Blooming period:
  Summer
Soil type:
  Well-drained open soil
Sun or Shade:
  Enjoys full sun
Hardiness:
  Minimum temp –29°C (–20°F)

Stipa gigantea • *Giant Feather Grass*

DESCRIPTION

This is a wide and varied grass (Poaceae) family genus of about 300 species of tufted, evergreen and deciduous grasses. Originally found on slopes in temperate and warm-temperate regions of the world, these grasses have made their way into ornamental gardens around the globe. They have fine-textured, linear, flat leaves that bear long panicles of feathery often fluffy flowerheads. Some species are grown for floral work. These plants are used widely in garden perennial borders and for roadside plantings. To thrive they need a fertile, medium to light soil in full sun. Propagation is by division in summer or seed can be sown in containers in spring.

S. *gigantea* is a striking and large perennial grass from Spain and Portugal, which forms a clump of green to grey-green foliage. Large loose panicles of flowers and seeds appear in spring, become golden, and persist through summer.

Species, variety or cultivar:
—
Other common names:
Giant Feather Grass,
Golden Oats
Height and spread:
2.4 x 1.2 m (8 x 4 ft)
Blooming period:
Spring
Soil type:
Fertile medium to light
soil
Sun or Shade:
Needs full sun
Hardiness:
Minimum temp −12°C
(10°F)

LEFT: This is an excellent alternative to pampas grass as a lawn specimen in small gardens, and perfect in a border or a gravel garden.

Stokesia laevis • *Stokes Aster*

DESCRIPTION

The only species in this genus, the Stokes aster was named after Dr Jonathan Stokes, an English doctor and botanist. It arrived in England in 1766 and was in vogue in Victorian times, especially as a cut flower. It later languished but is happily popular again.

S. *laevis* is found from South Carolina to Louisiana and northern Florida, USA. It is an upright plant with 15–20 cm (6–8 in) long, deep green, lance-shaped leaves at its base. Large cornflower-like heads to 10 cm (4 in) wide, solitary or in small clusters, usually mauve to purple, are borne in late summer to autumn.

Species, variety or cultivar:
–

Other common names:
Stokes Aster

Height and spread:
75 x 40 cm (30 x 16 in)

Blooming period:
Autumn

Soil type:
Light, free-draining soil

Sun or Shade:
Enjoys full sun and half-sun

Hardiness:
Minimum temp –23°C (–10°F)

Symphytum grandiflorum • *Comfrey*

DESCRIPTION

The 35 species of hardy perennials in this genus favour damp woodlands, streamsides and wasteland, and the plants are characterized by vigorous growth and prolific flowering. A basal rosette of coarse tapering leaves emerges from a fleshy taproot.

Comfrey has a long history of use to heal bruises and broken bones. If taken internally in quantity, it could be carcinogenic.

S. grandiflorum is a creeping rhizomatous perennial native to Turkey and eastern Europe with hairy oval leaves and pendulous tubular cream flowers, in many-flowered clusters, that are borne in spring to summer. Care should be taken as this species can be invasive.

Species, variety or cultivar:
–

Other common names:
Comfrey, Knitbone

Height and spread:
40 x 60 cm (16 x 24 in)

Blooming period:
Summer

Soil type:
Favours damp soil

Sun or Shade:
Likes full sun or partial shade

Hardiness:
Minimum temp –29°C (–20°F)

Tanacetum corymbosum

DESCRIPTION

This genus of about 70 annuals and perennials belonging to the daisy (Asteraceae) family originates in northern temperate regions. Flowers are daisy-like or rayless buttons, produced in a mass on vigorous plants of mounding, upright or shrubby habit. Colours are dominated by yellow, white and red. The genus name means 'immortality,' a reference to the flowers' habit of drying without wilting.

T. corymbosum is an attractive, clump-forming, woody perennial from southern and central Europe with aromatic, elliptical to oblong, mid-green leaves. Clusters of white flowerheads appear in early summer to late autumn. *T. c. subsp. clusii*, bears masses of white daisy-like flowers with drooping petals.

Species, variety or cultivar:
  subsp. clusii
Other common names:
  –
Height and spread:
  90 x 45 cm (36 x 18 in)
Blooming period:
  Summer to autumn
Soil type:
  Well-drained, poor to moderately fertile soil
Sun or Shade:
  Prefers full sun
Hardiness:
  Minimum temp –23°C (–10°F)

Tellima grandiflora • *Fringecups*

DESCRIPTION

There is just the one species of perennial herb in this genus that belongs to the saxifrage (Saxifragaceae) family. It is native to western North America, from California to Alaska, USA, where it is found in cool moist woodland and rocky areas. The plant forms spreading clumps of hairy, heart-shaped or round leaves, 5–10 cm (2–4 in) wide, that are lobed and toothed. They are tinted with purple in some forms. In summer, tall wiry flowering stems bear spikes of delicate creamy flowers tinged with green and red. The flowers deepen in colour as they age.

Species, variety or cultivar:
–
Other common names:
Fringecups
Height and spread:
60 x 60 cm (24 x 24 in)
Blooming period:
Summer
Soil type:
Moist, humus-rich soil
Sun or Shade:
Likes full shade
Hardiness:
Minimum temp –23°C (–10°F)

Thalictrum delavayi • *Meadow Rue*

DESCRIPTION

This genus of around 130 species of tuberous or rhizomatous perennials is found mainly in the northern temperate zone, in pink to mauve shades, but also white and yellow, the petal-less flowers sometimes gaining colour from their four or five petal-like sepals. The Romans favoured meadow rue as a medicinal plant and also attached superstitions to it.

T. delavayi is a perennial native to the Himalayas with dark-stemmed, blue-green, aquilegia- or maidenhair fern-like foliage. Erect showy heads of purple-pink, rarely white flowers, sepals similarly coloured, large and long-lasting, are borne in summer. The cultivar 'Hewitt's Double' has double flowers and is slightly shorter than the species.

Species, variety or cultivar:
  'Hewitt's Double'
Other common names:
  Meadow Rue
Height and spread:
  1.5 x 0.6 m (5 x 2 ft)
Blooming period:
  Summer
Soil type:
  Fertile, humus-rich, well-drained soil
Sun or Shade:
  Likes full sun or part-sun
Hardiness:
  Minimum temp −18°C (0°F)

Thymus serpyllum • *Creeping Thyme*

DESCRIPTION

Well known as the source of one of the most
widely used of the culinary herbs, this genus
of the mint (Lamiaceae) family is composed
of around 350 species. They occur in most
parts of Europe, temperate Asia and
northwest Africa but with the highest
concentration around the Mediterranean and
in the Middle East.

T. serpyllum is a variable wide mat-
forming perennial found from Greenland and
Scandinavia to northwestern Spain. It grows
close to ground from woody base and tiny
lavender-purple flowers bloom prolifically, in
early summer. 'Pink Chintz' has grey-green
leaves and pale salmon pink flowers.

Species, variety or cultivar:
  'Pink Chintz'
Other common names:
  Creeping Thyme, Mother-of-Thyme,
  Wild Thyme
Height and spread:
  10 x 90 cm (4 x 36 in)
Blooming period:
  Summer
Soil type:
  Light, rather gritty soil, enriched
  with humus for moisture retention
Sun or Shade:
  Enjoys full sun
Hardiness:
  Minimum temp –34°C (–30°F)

Tiarella • *Foamflower*

DESCRIPTION

This genus in the saxifrage (Saxifragaceae) family is made up of five perennials, four from North America and one found from the Himalayas to Japan which are very hardy, and easily grown in woodlands or perennial borders. The flower stems carry airy open racemes of tiny white and/or pink to red, 5-petalled flowers, in late spring and summer. Foliage and flower stems are covered in fine hairs.

North American foamflowers interbreed quite freely and intermediate forms are common. Hybridizers have developed these into a range of attractive garden forms, such as 'Dark Star', which has dark-centred bright green leaves, and pink-tinted white flowers.

Species, variety or cultivar:
 hybrid cultivar, 'Dark Star'
Other common names:
 Foamflower
Height and spread:
 45 x 50 cm (18 x 20 in)
Blooming period:
 Summer
Soil type:
 Humus-rich, moist, well-drained soil
Sun or Shade:
 Likes part- to full shade
Hardiness:
 Minimum temp –23°C (–10°F)

Tradescantia • *Spider Lily*

DESCRIPTION

This genus of around 70 species of annuals and perennials from the Americas is a member of the spiderwort (Commelinaceae) family. Tuberous or fibrous-rooted and often evergreen, they have rather succulent stems and fleshy, pointed elliptical, lance-shaped or narrow leaves.

The Andersoniana group includes hybrids of several species, not just one cross. Mainly derived from *T. virginiana*, it is a selection of mainly clump-forming hybrids with the narrow foliage and flowering habits of *T. virginiana*. One popular hybrid is 'Little Doll', which has very compact, bright green foliage and clusters of small, 3-petalled, soft mauve-blue flowers.

Species, variety or cultivar:
Andersoniana group, 'Little Doll'

Other common names:
Spider Lily, Spiderwort

Height and spread:
50 x 120 cm (20 x 48 in)

Blooming period:
Spring to summer

Soil type:
Moist, well-drained soil

Sun or Shade:
Prefers a sunny aspect

Hardiness:
Minimum temp –18°C (0°F)

Tricyrtis hirta • *Hairy Toad Lily*

DESCRIPTION

A graceful genus of 16 rhizomatous woodland perennials in the lily-of-the-valley (Convallariaceae) family, which occurs in moist woodlands and on mountains and cliffs from the eastern Himalayas to the Philippines, and in Japan and Taiwan. The star-, bell- or funnel-shaped flowers are terminal or in upper leaf axils and can be pure white, golden yellow, lavender or purple, usually spotted, with a somewhat waxen or iridescent quality.

T. hirta is an upright species from Japan with arching stems and slightly hairy soft green foliage. Striking pale lilac flowers, speckled with darker purple, bloom along the stems in the leaf axils, from early to mid-autumn.

Species, variety or cultivar:
 –
Other common names:
 Hairy Toad Lily
Height and spread:
 90 x 60 cm (36 x 24 in)
Blooming period:
 Autumn
Soil type:
 Moist, well-drained, humus-rich soil
Sun or Shade:
 Likes partial sun
Hardiness:
 Minimum temp –34°C (–30°F)

Trillium pusillum • *Dwarf Wake Robin*

DESCRIPTION

This group of 30 woodland perennials from North America and temperate Asia is the type genus for the wake-robin (Trilliaceae) family. Ranging from the tiny *T. rivale*, 5 cm (2 in) high, to species 60 cm (24 in) tall in flower, the genus is remarkably consistent in form.
The common name comes from their early flowering habit – the plant that wakes the robin in spring.

T. pusillum is a small woodland species from southeastern USA with narrow leaflets, to 5 cm (2 in) long, sometimes slightly blue-green. White flowers with nearly horizontal petals to 25 mm (1 in) long, and slightly larger conspicuous sepals appear in early spring.

Species, variety or cultivar:
–
Other common names:
Dwarf Wake Robin
Height and spread:
15 x 20 cm (6 x 8 in)
Blooming period:
Spring
Soil type:
Cool, moist, humus-rich, well-drained soil
Sun or Shade:
Enjoys part- or full shade
Hardiness:
Minimum temp –23°C (–10°F)

Trollius chinensis • *Globe Flower*

DESCRIPTION

There are about 31 species of perennial herbs in this genus, which is a member of the buttercup (Ranunculaceae) family. They are found in almost all northern temperate regions from the Himalayas to Turkey, China, Europe and North America. The roots are thick and fibrous, and the plants form basal tufts or rosettes of palmately-lobed and divided leaves with toothed edges. The flowers, often cupped, are up to 8 cm (3 in) wide, and have spirally arranged sepals and petals of white, yellow or orange, sometimes tinged with red or lilac. They grow in damp sunny meadows and on stream banks, often in heavy soils.

T. chinensis is a clumping species native to northern China with deeply-lobed finely-toothed leaves. Bowl-shaped golden yellow flowers with prominent stamens, on tall stems held well above foliage, are borne in summer. The cultivar 'Golden Queen' is an attractive deep orange-yellow.

LEFT: 'Golden Queen' is truly the queen of the buttercup family, having strongly erect stems requiring no staking, each stem topped by the largest, brightest tangerine blossoms which attract butterflies and bees.

Species, variety or cultivar:
'Golden Queen'
Other common names:
Globe Flower
Height and spread:
90 x 45 cm (36 x 18 in)
Blooming period:
Spring
Soil type:
Permanently moist soil, or boggy areas beside water
Sun or Shade:
Either full sun or part-shade
Hardiness:
Minimum temp –29°C (–20°F)

Tropaeolum polyphyllum • *Wreath Nasturtium*

DESCRIPTION

This genus of over 80 species of sometimes tuberous annuals and perennials is found from southern Mexico to the southern tip of South America. Though variable, the foliage is often shield-shaped, and the genus name comes from the Greek *tropaion*, 'trophy,' a term used for the tree trunk on which were hung the shields and helmets of defeated enemies.

T. polyphyllum is an annual or perennial trailer or climber from Chile and Argentina, with grey-green to blue-green 5- to 7-lobed leaves; some forms have near-circular leaves. Clusters of bright yellow funnel-shaped flowers, partly contained within large calyces, appear in summer.

Species, variety or cultivar:
–
Other common names:
Wreath Nasturtium
Height and spread:
3 x 3 m (10 x 10 ft)
Blooming period:
Summer
Soil type:
Moist, well-drained soil
Sun or Shade:
Plant in full sun or half-sun
Hardiness:
Minimum temp –12°C (10°F)

Tulbaghia simmleri • *Pink Agapanthus*

DESCRIPTION

These bulbous perennials come from summer-rainfall areas in southern Africa, and those in cultivation adapt well to irrigated beds in dry-summer climates. The umbels of starry flowers are held well above the leaves. Many carry a persistent stale garlic scent when crushed. The flowers of these garden-grown members are dainty to look at and perform well over extended periods. Some will even put on two flowery displays in a single year, depending on local conditions and the mood of the moment. *T. simmleri* is from South Africa and has comparatively broad grey-green leaves. Clusters of up to 40 scented mauve flowers appear from spring to summer.

Species, variety or cultivar:
–
Other common names:
Pink Agapanthus, Sweet Garlic
Height and spread:
60 x 30 cm (24 x 12 in)
Blooming period:
Spring to summer
Soil type:
Well-drained soil
Sun or Shade:
Needs full sun
Hardiness:
Minimum temp –12°C (10°F)

Verbascum adzharicum • *Moth Mullein*

DESCRIPTION

This figwort (Scrophulariaceae) family genus of some 300 species includes cultivated plants and many that have become weeds outside their natural Eurasian and North African range. The commonly cultivated species usually form basal rosettes of large elliptic leaves, often heavily veined and sometimes felted. Tall upright flower spikes emerge from the rosettes, carrying massed, small, 5-petalled flowers, usually in white, yellow or pink to lavender shades. Verbascum was described by the Roman writer Pliny as attractive to moths: he called them moth mulleins. It also featured as a protection against evil in Greek legends and was used as an everyday medicinal plant to treat a variety of ills.

Species, variety or cultivar:
–
Other common names:
Moth Mullein, Mullein
Height and spread:
90 x 40 cm (36 x 16 in)
Blooming period:
Summer
Soil type:
Light, gritty, free-draining soil
Sun or Shade:
Likes full sun to partial shade
Hardiness:
Minimum temp –34°C (–30°F)

V. adzharicum is a summer-flowering biennial or short-lived perennial endemic to the forests and alpine meadows of the Transcaucasus. It has rosettes of felted grey-green leaves and leafy flower stems that bear short spikes of bright yellow flowers with purple filaments from early summer.

Verbascum • *Moth Mullein*

DESCRIPTION

There are some 300 species included in this Eurasian and North African genus, which has basal rosettes of large elliptic leaves. Tall upright flower spikes carry masses of small 5-petalled flowers. Most prefer a sunny position with light, gritty, free-draining soil. They can tolerate summer drought but need moisture until after flowering.

Moth mulleins hybridize freely, and British breeders in particular have produced a range of hybrids that combine lush velvety foliage with beautifully shaded flowers. Some of the best include members of the Cotswold Group such as 'Cotswold Beauty', which has buff to apricot-pink flowers, and purple-pink anthers.

Species, variety or cultivar:
hybrid cultivar, 'Cotswold Beauty'
Other common names:
Moth Mullein, Mullein
Height and spread:
120 x 50 cm (48 x 20 in)
Blooming period:
Summer
Soil type:
Light, gritty, free-draining soil
Sun or Shade:
Enjoys full sun to partial shade
Hardiness:
Minimum temp –23°C (–10°F)

Verbena bonariensis • *Helmet Flower*

DESCRIPTION

This member of the self-named vervain (Verbenaceae) family contains 250 species of annuals, perennials and subshrubs native to tropical and subtropical America. The plants are sprawling to erect; leaves are opposite and variously divided. The terminal flowerheads range from narrow and overlapping to broader, rounder clusters. Individual flowers are tubular with flaring, sometimes notched, lobes. Flowers come in shades of purple, pink, red and white.

V. bonariensis is from South America and is a robust perennial often grown as an annual. Erect, markedly square, rough-textured stems are sparsely covered with lance-shaped, serrated-edged leaves. Tiny purple flowers in flat-topped clusters are borne from summer to autumn.

Species, variety or cultivar:
–

Other common names:
Purple Top, South African Vervain, Tall Verbena

Height and spread:
1.5 x 0.6 m (5 x 2 ft)

Blooming period:
Summer to autumn

Soil type:
Moderately fertile, moist but well-drained soil

Sun or Shade:
Prefers full sun

Hardiness:
Minimum temp −18°C (0°F)

Verbena hastata • *Blue Vervain*

DESCRIPTION

There are 250 species in this genus from tropical and subtropical America. The common name vervain comes from the Celtic ferfaen, 'to drive away a stone,' a reference to the use of *V. officinalis* as a cure for bladder infections.

It was also a supposed aphrodisiac and cure-all for problems ranging from snakebites to heart disease.

V. hastata is native to eastern and central USA, and is a perennial with stiff upright stems and lance-shaped, toothed, roughened leaves. Small violet-blue flowers in spiky clusters appear in summer to autumn. The species is used in herbal remedies for a range of complaints.

Species, variety or cultivar:
   –
Other common names:
   Blue Vervain, Simpler's Joy
Height and spread:
   101 x 40 cm (40 x 16 in)
Blooming period:
   Summer to autumn
Soil type:
   Moderately fertile, moist but well-drained soil
Sun or Shade:
   Likes full sun
Hardiness:
   Minimum temp –40°C (–40°F)

Veronica gentianoides • *Birdseye*

DESCRIPTION

This figwort (Scrophulariaceae) family genus of 250 species of annuals and perennials is widespread in northern temperate zones. Most are creeping mat-forming plants that sometimes strike root as they spread. Their leaves tend to be small, oval to lance-shaped, often shallowly toothed and rarely pinnately lobed.

V. gentianoides is a spreading Caucasian and western Asian perennial that forms dense clumps of upright stems with narrow, toothed, pointed oval leaves and grows to nearly 8 cm (3 in) long at the base of the clump. Erect spikes of usually pale blue flowers up to 30 cm (12 in) long are borne in summer.

Species, variety or cultivar:
    –
Other common names:
    Birdseye, Speedwell
Height and spread:
    60 x 60 cm (24 x 24 in)
Blooming period:
    Spring to summer
Soil type:
    Moist, well-drained soil
Sun or Shade:
    Easily grown in full sun to half-sun
Hardiness:
    Minimum temp –34°C (–30°F)

Veronica spicata • *Birdseye*

DESCRIPTION

Of the 250 species in this genus, a few have solitary flowers, but more often they have many-flowered upright spikes which develop in spring and summer. Probably named in honour of St Veronica, or because the floral markings of some species resemble the

marks left on Veronica's sacred handkerchief or veil, with which she wiped Christ's face as he carried the cross.

V. spicata is a European summer-flowering perennial that forms a clump of erect stems with downy, finely toothed, narrow lance-shaped leaves. Terminal spikes are densely packed with deep blue flowers. Its cultivars include 'Icicle', which has long spikes of white flowers.

Species, variety or cultivar:
  'Icicle'
Other common names:
  Birdseye, Speedwell
Height and spread:
  60 x 80 cm (24 x 32 in)
Blooming period:
  Spring to summer
Soil type:
  Moist, well-drained soil
Sun or Shade:
  Likes both full and partial sun
Hardiness:
  Minimum temp –40°C (–40°F)

Veronicastrum virginicum • *Blackroot*

DESCRIPTION

This genus of two upright perennials, members of the figwort (Scrophulariaceae) family, is native to northeastern Asia and northeastern North America. The plants have whorls of simple leaves and a terminal raceme of spikes of flowers with a calyx with four to five lobes, and a saucer-shaped corolla with two stamens.

V. virginicum is a perennial, native to northeastern America, with whorls of four to seven simple, smooth, sword-shaped, serrated leaves. Dense, slender spikes, to 30 cm (12 in) tall, of tiny pale blue or white flowers appear in summer. *V. v. var. sibiricum*, is characterized by narrow spikes of lilac flowers.

Species, variety or cultivar:
var. sibiricum

Other common names:
Blackroot, Bowman's Root, Culver's Root

Height and spread:
1.8 x 0.9 m (6 x 3 ft)

Blooming period:
Summer

Soil type:
Moist, humus-rich soil

Sun or Shade:
Will grow in full or half-sun

Hardiness:
Minimum temp –40°C (–40°F)

Vinca minor • *Creeping Myrtle*

DESCRIPTION

This genus of seven species of evergreen ground-covering perennials found in woodland areas of North Africa, central Asia and Europe, is part of the dogbane (Apocynaceae) family. Star-shaped flowers appear from spring to late autumn and will vary in colour from dark purple to blue and white.

V. minor is from Europe, southern Russia, and northern Caucasus and is a tight mat-forming, evergreen perennial with dark green leaves, 5 cm (2 in) long. Star-shaped violet-blue flowers, 3 cm (1¼ in) across, appear from early spring to mid-autumn. Ideal for hanging baskets. 'Atropurpurea' has dark plum coloured flowers.

Species, variety or cultivar:
  'Atropurpurea'
Other common names:
  Creeping Myrtle
Height and spread:
  20 x 300 cm (8 x 120 in)
Blooming period:
  Spring to autumn
Soil type:
  Free-draining light soil
Sun or Shade:
  Copes with both full sun and full shade
Hardiness:
  Minimum temp –18°C (0°F)

Viola cornuta • *Bedding Pansy*

DESCRIPTION

Viola includes some 500 species of annuals, perennials and subshrubs found in all the world's temperate zones from the mountains of New Zealand to the subarctic.

V. cornuta is native to the Pyrenees and northern Spain and is a late spring- to summer-flowering, rhizome-rooted perennial, initially prostrate then more mounding. It has oval, shallowly toothed leaves and spurred, broad-petalled, violet flowers with darker veining and a yellow centre. There are also many mixed colour seedling strains, such as the Princess Series. 'Princess Lavender and Yellow' is an attractive violet purple with purple-veined white inner petals, and a yellow centre.

Species, variety or cultivar:
  Princess Series, 'Princess Lavender and Yellow'

Other common names:
  Bedding Pansy, Horned Violet

Height and spread:
  30 x 35 cm (12 x 14 in)

Blooming period:
  Spring to summer

Soil type:
  Moist, well-drained soil

Sun or Shade:
  Likes full sun to part-sun

Hardiness:
  Minimum temp −18°C (0°F)

Viola pyrenaica • *Pyrenean Violet*

DESCRIPTION

There are over 500 species of violas, and all have remarkably similarly shaped 5-petalled flowers, with the lower petal often carrying dark markings. White, yellow and purple predominate but the flowers occur in every colour, at least among the garden forms. The plants have been used medicinally in several ways, and also symbolically: *V. tricolour* was a symbol of Athens and was also used by Napoleon.

V. pyrenaica is a small spring-flowering perennial found in southern Europe from Spain to Bulgaria. It develops into a clump of broad, shallowly toothed, pointed oval leaves, with short-spurred purple flowers, to around 18 mm (¾ in) wide.

Species, variety or cultivar:
  –
Other common names:
  Pyrenean Violet
Height and spread:
  10 x 20 cm (4 x 8 in)
Blooming period:
  Spring to autumn
Soil type:
  Moist, well-drained soil
Sun or Shade:
  Needs part- to full shade
Hardiness:
  Minimum temp −23°C (−10°F)

Waldsteinia ternata

DESCRIPTION

There are six species of creeping fleshy-stemmed perennials in this genus, which belongs to the rose (Rosaceae) family. They are native to northern temperate regions where they are inhabitants of woodland areas. Plants form low mats of lobed and toothed leaves that are similar to those of the related strawberry and cinquefoil (Potentilla).

W. ternata is found from Europe to China and Japan and is a vigorous ground-covering plant with dark green, 3-lobed, toothed, somewhat hairy leaves. Yellow, saucer-shaped, 5-petalled flowers nearly 18 mm (¾ in) wide, are borne in groups of three to seven in spring and summer.

Species, variety or cultivar:
–
Other common names:
–
Height and spread:
15 x 60 cm (6 x 24 in)
Blooming period:
Spring to summer
Soil type:
Moist, well-drained soils
Sun or Shade:
Prefers partial shade
Hardiness:
Minimum temp –40°C (–40°F)

Yucca filamentosa • *Adam's Needle*

DESCRIPTION

Native to dry regions of North and Central America and the West Indies, there are about 40 species in this genus within the Agavaceae family, which include evergreen herbaceous perennials, as well as trees and shrubs. Bell- to cup-shaped flowers are held on usually erect panicles.

Y. filamentosa is a bushy yucca found in eastern USA. Usually trunkless, it forms multiple suckering heads of 75 cm (30 in) long, filamentous, blue-green leaves. Flower stems up to 3 m (10 ft) tall bearing masses of pendulous cream flowers, appear in summer. 'Bright Edge' is a dwarf cultivar with yellow-edged foliage.

Species, variety or cultivar:
  'Bright Edge'
Other common names:
  Adam's Needle
Height and spread:
  0.9 x 1.5 m (3 x 5 ft)
Blooming period:
  Summer
Soil type:
  Loamy soil with good drainage
Sun or Shade:
  Needs full sun
Hardiness:
  Minimum temp –23°C (–10°F)

Zantedeschia aethiopica • *Arum Lily*

DESCRIPTION

The large calla lily (*Z. aethiopica*) is a plant that polarizes opinions. Some gardeners love it, while others can't abide its funereal associations. Widely naturalized in mild areas, this evergreen or semi-evergreen species develops large rhizomes and can form impressive clumps of long-stemmed, 30–60 cm (12–24 in) long, arrowhead-shaped leaves. Tall flower stems are topped with a white spathe, to 25 cm (10 in) long, around a yellow spadix. 'Crowborough' grows to 90 cm (3 ft) tall, has a small greenish spathe, and can be invasive, so care should be taken. Named after Italian botanist Giovanni Zantedeschi (1773–1846).

Species, variety or cultivar:
'Crowborough'
Other common names:
Arum Lily, Calla Lily
Height and spread:
90 x 90 cm (36 x 36 in)
Blooming period:
Spring to autumn
Soil type:
Any garden soil that does not dry out
Sun or Shade:
Likes part- to full shade
Hardiness:
Minimum temp –12°C (10°F)

Zantedeschia • *Arum Lily*

DESCRIPTION

This arum (Araceae) family genus comprises six species of rhizome-rooted perennials from southern Africa. The flower spathe is funnel-shaped and tapers to a drip-tip, while

the spadix may be enclosed within the spathe or protrudes slightly. Although the white calla is the best known, modern hybrids cover a wide colour range. Both leaves and the flowers are supported by strong stalks.

Developed through crossing most of the smaller species, the hybrid cultivars are generally quite compact. Typically they have white-spotted leaves and sturdy flower stems with showy spathes. 'Flame' has red-flecked yellow spathes deepening in colour with age.

Species, variety or cultivar:
  hybrid cultivar, 'Flame'
Other common names:
  Arum Lily, Calla Lily
Height and spread:
  60 x 60 cm (2 x 2 ft)
Blooming period:
  Spring to autumn
Soil type:
  Any garden soil that does not dry out
Sun or Shade:
  Prefers part- to full shade
Hardiness:
  Minimum temp –7°C (20°F)

Zigadenus fremontii • *Star Lily*

DESCRIPTION

This genus of 18 bulbous or rhizomatous perennial herbs, members of the lily (Liliaceae) family, is native to temperate North America and northern Asia. All members of the genus are highly poisonous to humans and livestock.

Z. *fremontii* is a perennial herb found from southern Oregon to northern Baja California, USA. It grows from spherical bulbs, 25–30 mm (1–1¼ in) in diameter, and has narrow, slightly rough, curved leaves, to 60 cm (24 in) long, which grow from a central base. Open spreading panicles of off-white or ivory flowers appear in summer, on smooth stems 40–90 cm (16–36 in) tall.

Species, variety or cultivar:
–

Other common names:
Star Lily, Star Zygadene

Height and spread:
90 x 12 cm (36 x 5 in)

Blooming period:
Summer

Soil type:
Moist, well-drained soil

Sun or Shade:
Prefers a position in full sun

Hardiness:
Minimum temp –29°C (–20°F)

Zingiber spectabile • *Beehive Ginger*

DESCRIPTION

This group of approximately 60 herbaceous and
evergreen rhizomatous, clumping, perennial herbs
gives its name to the ginger (Zingiberaceae)
family. Originating in Indomalaysia, East Asia and
northern Australia, most are frost tender,
although some species prove surprisingly hardy in
temperate gardens. Most prefer nutrient-rich,
well-drained, moist soil and full sun to part-shade
in warm, humid conditions.

Z. spectabile is from Malaysia and has long,
deep green leaves with paler, downy undersides. It
has long cylindrical inflorescences of yellow bracts
turning to scarlet, and small creamy white flowers
that have a 2-lobed dark purple lip with yellow
spots, are borne in late summer.

Species, variety or cultivar:
–

Other common names:
Beehive Ginger

Height and spread:
2 x 0.9 m (7 x 3 ft)

Blooming period:
Summer

Soil type:
Nutrient-rich, well-drained,
moist soil

Sun or Shade:
Likes full sun and part-shade

Hardiness:
Minimum temp –7°C (20°F)

Index *of Latin names*

Index *of Common names*

Credits

Text and photographs by arrangement with Global Book Publishing Pty LTD.